Volume 17, Number 1, 2005

Journal of Public Relations Research

A Quarterly Publication of the Public Relations Division of the Association for Education in Journalism and Mass Communication

Special Issue:
Public Relations From the Margins
Mary Anne Moffitt

T0371633

SUBSCRIBER INFORMATION

Journal of Public Relations Research is published quarterly by Lawrence Erlbaum Associates, Inc., 10 Industrial Avenue, Mahwah, NJ 07430–2262. Subscriptions for Volume 17, 2005 are available on a calendar-year basis only. Direct subscribers send changes to Lawrence Erlbaum Associates, Inc., at above address. Address changes should include the mailing label or a facsimile. Claims for missing issues cannot be honored beyond 4 months after mailing date. Duplicate copies cannot be sent to replace issues not delivered due to failure to notify publisher of change of address.

Individual rates: **Print-*Plus*-Online:** $60.00 in US/Canada, and $90.00 outside US/Canada. Institutional rates: **Print-Only:** $505.00 in US/Canada, and $535.00 outside US/Canada. **Online-Only:** $480.00 in US/Canada and outside US/Canada. **Print-*Plus*-Online:** $530.00 in US/Canada, and $560.00 outside US/Canada. Visit LEA's Web site at http://www.erlbaum.com to view a free sample.

Order subscriptions through the Journal Subscription Department, Lawrence Erlbaum Associates, Inc., 10 Industrial Avenue, Mahwah, NJ 07430–2262.

This journal is abstracted and indexed in *ComIndex; ComAbstracts; Communication Abstracts; Communication Institute for Online Scholarship; Index to Journals in Mass Communication; PsycINFO;* and *EBSCOhost Products*.

Microform copies of this journal are available through ProQuest Information and Learning, P.O. Box 1346, Ann Arbor, MI 48106–1346. For more information, call 1–800–521–0600 x2888.

JOURNAL OF PUBLIC RELATIONS RESEARCH, *17*(1), 1
Copyright © 2005, Lawrence Erlbaum Associates, Inc.

EDITOR'S NOTE

I extend my deepest gratitude to all of the people who made possible this special issue of the *Journal of Public Relations Research.* Guest editor Mary Anne Moffitt deserves a special thank you for proposing the idea and managing all aspects of the review process independently. She also assembled an impressive editorial board of scholars who culled from many fine submissions the outstanding pieces of research featured here. Mary Anne and I are indebted to these reviewers: David Allen, Joseph Blaney, Denise Bostdorff, Jeffrey Courtright, Bryan Crable, Kathleen German, Lawrence Grossberg, Keith Hearit, Robert Heath, Angela Jerome, Dean Kazoleas, Dean Kruckeberg, Jacquie L'Etang, Shirely Leitch, John McHale, Dan Millar, David Miller, Priscilla Murphy, Lana Rakow, Donald Rybacki, and Joseph Zompetti.

I hope you will agree with me that this special issue represents a significant turning point in the evolution of public relations scholarship. When a critical mass of scholars within a field begin to critique its dominant paradigm and first generation theories, a new level of insight becomes possible. At the same time, the impact of this first generation paradigm and its theoretical assumptions is underscored because, as Moffit points out in her preface, the scholarship of these first generation theorists provides the epicenter around which critical research finds its voice. Within the dialogue and debate, we discover the exciting and profound state of public relations scholarship that this journal is uniquely suited to showcase.

—Linda Childers Hon

JOURNAL OF PUBLIC RELATIONS RESEARCH, *17*(1), 3–4

Comments on Special Issue Public Relations From the Margins

Mary Anne Moffitt

Editor, Special Issue

The articles in this special issue address some of the key issues facing the research and the practice of public relations today. These studies acknowledge that traditional, mainstream public relations research argues for excellence in public relations according to the symmetry model and to considerations of the dominant coalition controlling the organization. What are proposed in this special journal issue are responses to these assumptions and suggestions that what might be just as important to consider are the sociopolitical context that surrounds the organization and the notion that power exists in other sites besides the dominant coalition. These articles are, in essence, a conversation, a give-and-take between established beliefs and new possibilities for understanding public relations. Furthermore, these studies' important theoretical contributions are their expression in real life situations and case study applications.

Bruce Berger opens the conversation by reexamining concepts of organizational power and the dominant coalition. Berger argues for the recognition of other sites of organizational power and proposes that, given typical male control and power within the dominant coalition, organizational power is often played out as a gendered dialectic.

Frank Durham offers structuration as a theoretical perspective in addition to mainstream perspectives in public relations research. Durham wants public relations to quit reifying the top-down mentality of organizational power and consider, instead, social patterns for structures, rules, and actors who have power in the public relations function.

Requests for reprints should be sent to Mary Anne Moffitt, Department of Communication, Box 4480, Normal, IL 61790–4480. Email: mamoffi@ilstu.edu

Judy Motion and C. Kay Weaver react to the dominant, managerial perspective and also examine the sociopolitical context. Motion and Weaver explain through their critical theoretical perspective how social discourses serve as loci of power in their circulation of public relations ideas, messages, and strategies.

The final study also uses a critical framework for examining organizational and public relations power through the lens of hegemony and Habermas's communication action. Juliet Roper argues that power is constantly negotiated through three dominant discourses of organizations (Economy), public policy (State), and the social formation (Civil Society). She explains the rise in recent years of organizational power along with its respective technological developments to dictate governmental policy and policy toward civil society.

JOURNAL OF PUBLIC RELATIONS RESEARCH, *17*(1), 5–28

Power Over, Power With, and Power to Relations: Critical Reflections on Public Relations, the Dominant Coalition, and Activism

Bruce K. Berger

Department of Advertising and Public Relations,
College of Communication
University of Alabama

Symmetrical public relations theory acknowledges primacy of the dominant coalition in making organizational decisions and influencing public relations practices but reveals little about this powerful inner circle. Drawing from interviews with 21 public relations executives, this article opens up the dominant coalition and reveals its complex power relationships and a matrix of constraints that undermine and limit the function, rendering it difficult for practitioners to do the "right" thing, even if they want to. If public relations is to better serve society, professionals and academics may need to embrace an activist role and combine advocacy of shared power with activism in the interest of shared power.

The dominant coalition is a pivotal concept in mainstream public relations theory. Membership in this powerful decision-making group advances the profession's status and allows practitioners to help organizations solve problems and become more socially responsible (Broom & Dozier, 1985; J. E. Grunig & Hunt, 1984; Plowman, 1998). A key assumption in this perspective is that practitioners will do the "right" thing once inside the dominant coalition—they will or will try to represent the voices and interests of others and to shape an organization's ideology and decisions to benefit the profession, the organization, and greater society (J. E. Grunig & L. A. Grunig, 1989; L. A. Grunig, 1992).

Requests for reprints should be sent to Bruce K. Berger, Department of Advertising and Public Relations, College of Communication, University of Alabama, Box 870172, Tuscaloosa, AL 35487–0172. Email: berger@apr.ua.edu

Consistent with the theme of this special issue, I speak from the margins by challenging this assumption and "opening up" the dominant coalition. I argue that this assumption glosses complex power relations and structural practices and processes inside dominant coalitions that render it difficult for practitioners to do the "right" thing—even if they want to. Following a review of the literature I demystify the dominant coalition by examining who is inside it, where and how it operates, and the decisions and deliverables it produces. My analysis takes the form of six propositions—grounded in interviews with 21 public relations executives—that bear implications for practitioners and provide a framework for examining three relations of power in the dominant coalition.

Power over relations refer to a traditional dominance model where decision making is characterized by control, instrumentalism, and self-interest. Public relations is an influence variable in this view. *Power with* relations reflect an empowerment model where dialogue, inclusion, negotiation, and shared power guide decision making. Here, public relations is a relational variable. An ongoing, gendered dialectic is seen to occur between power over and power with relations inside the dominant coalition. *Power to* relations represent forms of resistance that public relations practitioners may use to try to counter a dominance model. Although little explored (Weaver, 2001), practitioner resistance and activism may offer best hope for professionals to do the right thing and to actualize the possibilities of a practice serving the interests and voices of many.

There is little doubt that public relations has effectively served capitalism and powerful economic producers for many years, but whether it has served or can serve stakeholders and society as well from inside or outside the dominant coalition is a contested issue (Motion & Leitch, 1996; Weaver, 2001). My critique suggests this is unlikely unless (a) public relations theory provides a fuller, more illuminating account of power relations; and (b) public relations professionals and teachers become more astute political players and engaged activists.

THE DOMINANT COALITION AND PUBLIC RELATIONS—THE LITERATURE

The dominant coalition has its roots in the work of organizational theorists (L. A. Grunig, 1992). Cyert and March (1963) first theorized that a coalition of individuals, including top management, set organizational goals, and the values of this group shaped organizational behaviors. Thompson (1967) used the term *inner circle* to refer to this group of influentials. Hage (1980) argued that the dominant coalition was an outgrowth of increased environmental complexity: Specialized teams and joint decision making were necessary because organizations and the environment were too large for one individual to control. However, the dominant coalition shaped organizational action more so than did the environment (Allen, 1979). Mintzberg (1983) constructed a typology of internal and external coalitions, including public relations as a support function whose source of power was its expertise in communications.

The dominant coalition reflects a power–control perspective in organizations (Child, 1972; Pfeffer, 1981; Simon, 1976). Members of the dominant coalition draw power from a variety of sources—authority, coercion, charisma, expertise, information, reward, and sanctions—to influence decisions (Bachrach & Lawler, 1980; French & Raven, 1959). Power holders compete to shape organizational decisions, resource allocations, and interpretations, and these ongoing conflicts produce organizational structure (Lauzen & Dozier, 1992). On this view, power is an individual attribute or capacity, although it can be considered as departmental or organizational as well (L. A. Grunig, 1992).

Schneider (1985) incorporated this perspective and the dominant coalition into public relations research by linking the function of public relations to organizational environment (external stakeholders) and internal decision making (Lauzen & Dozier, 1992). Dozier, L. A. Grunig, and J. E. Grunig (1995) found that decisions of the dominant coalition influenced the practice of public relations in the organization. However, having identified the dominant coalition as a locus of organizational power, public relations theorists and researchers confronted a major problem: Practitioners were seldom members of the inner circle (L. A. Grunig, 1992).

This problem has been approached largely in two ways: Researchers have identified what practitioners need to do to gain a seat in the dominant coalition, and they have assembled arguments about the value of the public relations perspective in this role. Practitioners are believed to be excluded from the inner circle because (a) management does not understand or appreciate the public relations role (e.g., Burger, 1983; Strenski, 1980); or (b) practitioner skills, experience, and education are deficient (Dozier et al., 1995; Ehling, 1992; J. E. Grunig, 1992).

A major line of research in this regard has differentiated the technical versus manager role (Broom & Dozier, 1985, 1986; Dozier, 1983, 1984, 1992). As technicians, practitioners carry out production activities (e.g., writing and design work) but are not engaged in policy decision making. Managers possess similar technical skills but also have problem-solving and strategic-thinking capabilities and are accountable for results. Public relations professionals who possess such managerial skills, sufficient experience, and a managerial perspective are therefore more likely to make it into the inner circle.

The second approach has advocated the value of public relations expertise in dominant coalitions. Simply put, organizations benefit from including public relations managers in the dominant coalition because they possess conflict resolution skills (J. E. Grunig & L. A. Grunig, 1992; Plowman, 1998) that are growing in demand in a complex organizational world (Gossen & Sharp, 1987; Roloff, 1987). More important, public relations managers can help organizations practice the two-way symmetrical model of public relations, which helps organizations balance self-interests with the interests of others through meaningful, dialogic relationships with publics (Dozier et al., 1995; J. E. Grunig, 1992, 2001).

Summarizing, then, the dominant coalition is a pivotal concept in public relations theory. This group of powerful insiders makes strategic choices, allocates resources, and influences public relations practices. Public relations managers therefore must be part of the dominant coalition if they are to favorably influence organizational choices, ideology, and practices (Daugherty, 2001). In doing so, public relations helps organizations manage their social responsibility obligations and build substantive relationships with others (J. E. Grunig, 2001).

Implicit in this theorizing is the assumption that public relations managers who ascend to the inner circle will operate on the basis of a relational or symmetrical (excellence) world view and do, or try to do, the right thing in the interests of the profession, organization, and society. As L. A. Grunig (1992) put it in more qualified language, "Presumably [public relations professionals] ... would appreciate the point of view both of their employers and of their relevant external publics" (p. 491). This assumption and the dominant coalition need to be opened up.

A CLOSER LOOK INSIDE THE DOMINANT COALITION

Rich in theorizing the value of public relations to the dominant coalition, the literature is meager regarding what happens in the group, how it happens, and what the implications are for public relations managers. For purposes here, then, let us imagine that a public relations manager has gained a seat in the dominant coalition and wants to do the right thing. What does the manager encounter in the inner circle? How do things happen there? What constraints on public relations exist, or, conversely, what opportunities for action are presented?

In the following sections I propose a set of answers to these questions, but it is important to first disclose my limitations in doing so. As a critical theorist, I am interested in the dominant coalition because it is a locus of organizational power and communication. I am especially interested in how power in this group both constrains, and creates opportunities for, public relations professionals to participate and try to do the right thing. I am also concerned with forms of professional resistance and political activism in the field. Like Cheney and Christensen (2001), I believe that "theoretical-practical reflection can and should be directed toward evocation, provocation, enlightenment and social betterment" (p. 168).

My interpretation of the dominant coalition and power relations reflects biases growing out of 20 years of professional public relations experience with two large corporations. With the first company I was sometimes involved in the dominant coalition, most often during crises. In the second corporation I was the senior public relations officer and a "regular" member of the dominant coalition. I cannot fully set aside these experiences, but I can temper them with the views and experiences of others, and three books have been especially valuable in this regard.

Spicer (1997) provided a rare but important political perspective on public relations, one intended to help practitioners operate in their organizations' political networks. Jackall (1988) provided a fascinating if discouraging look at how public relations professionals and other managers manipulate meanings to serve the interests of their bosses, their organizations, and themselves. Bologh (1990), a sociologist and feminist, was not writing about public relations in this work, but her critique of Max Weber's political realism provided an important framework for considering gender implications of power over and power with relations.

I also turn to public relations executives who are insiders. Through my work and memberships in professional associations, I have discussed power issues with dozens of practitioners and conducted in-depth interviews with 21 public relations executives (17 men, 4 women) who are, or were, members of dominant coalitions in major corporations and who possess extensive experience in the field. Communication executives are centrally concerned with power relations in their organizations, and the interviews explored their perceptions of the dominant coalition; corporate power structures and relations; constraints on, and opportunities for, public relations advocacy; and forms of public relations resistance and activism, among other related topics. All executives participated in at least one interview of 60 min or more, while 6 executives completed two interviews, and 2 executives completed three interviews, for a total of more than 40 hr of in-depth interviews. The interviews provide a qualitative foundation for this article and help mitigate some of my biases.

In this section I draw from these interviews and the literature to open up the dominant coalition. I develop six propositions about dominant coalitions (in large, complex organizations) that bear implications for public relations professionals and practices. The propositions provide a more detailed picture of the dominant coalition and establish a framework for analyzing extant power relationships in the inner circle.

> Proposition 1: The existence of a single, all-prevailing dominant coalition is a myth: Power relations occur in multiple dominant coalitions in large organizations.

According to public relations executives interviewed, multiple-dominant coalitions—defined as groups that make significant strategic and resource allocation decisions—operate in their organizations. The company's board of directors (BOD) was consistently identified as the "leading" dominant coalition. However, as several vice presidents (VPs) noted, this role may be more ceremonial than strategic because the BOD is seldom directly involved in day-to-day strategic decision making and often "rubber stamps" the recommendations of the chief executive officer (CEO) or president. None of the executives interviewed were members of the BOD, although most had delivered briefings to the group regarding crisis activities or various program initiatives.

According to the public relations executives, most of the decision-making struggles occur beneath the BOD level among multiple-dominant coalitions. These are the intersecting power groups—loosely or tightly coupled—where public relations managers seek and are sometimes active in strategic roles. Some of these coalitions or power groups are relatively fixed and formal in nature, whereas others are more ad hoc and contingency based. For example, one relatively formal dominant coalition generally reviews and approves annual budgets and plans. At the corporate level, this group is likely to include the CEO, chief finance officer (CFO), president, financial VP, and perhaps some functional leaders. The comments of one public relations VP of a large healthcare company reflect the sentiments of most of those interviewed about this particular coalition:

> The budget and plan review committee has significant power because it decides, yea or nay, on budget requests and strategic plans. I'm always involved in this group in terms of presenting our proposal and advocating for it. But I have no real voting power over what ultimately does or doesn't get approved. Neither do most other functional heads. We present, we argue, we lobby after meetings, and then we mostly wait. The CEO, CFO, and maybe the financial VP, they take the numbers, decide how to bless them, and then we're told our allocation some time later. So, we have an advocacy position in the group, but we don't really have admission to that small decision-making group within the group.

According to participants, other "formal" dominant coalitions that often involve public relations include crisis and safety committees, corporate foundation or philanthropy boards, and public affairs management teams. Most of those interviewed said that roles in these groups are reasonably well established and involve advocacy, recognized professional expertise, and some involvement in decision making. Nearly all of the interviewees indicated that public relations played an important role in most ad hoc dominant coalitions, especially crisis management teams. They indicated that such teams were central arenas for advocating effective public relations approaches that were highly sensitive to groups of stakeholders and incorporated the interests and perspectives of others. One VP described this role as follows:

> I've always felt our executives pay a lot more attention to public relations during a crisis. Some of my colleagues say this is because they're looking for a scapegoat—and PR fits the bill. But during a crisis you have full executive attention, which is so hard to get otherwise, given the pace of our business. Your point of view may not always win out, but it will get expressed and listened to. And if the group takes your advice and it turns out well, your contribution isn't forgotten; you've accumulated some future influence.

Proposition 2:   Venues for dominant coalitions shift back and forth from the
formal to informal, making ongoing participation difficult.

Many of the public relations executives indicated that venues for dominant coalitions often shift from formal to informal settings, effectively closing out or reducing the participation of public relations or other functions in the coalitions.
Formal venues refer to scheduled meetings at designated sites where all members
of a dominant coalition discuss and attempt to resolve issues. Informal venues are
unannounced meetings of only a few coalition members who meet alone or in
out-of-the-way places to continue discussion and make decisions, for example,
airplanes, closed video conferencing, golf outings, and so forth. As a result, decision making is highly fluid and renders effective participation more difficult. One
public relations director in the computer industry captured this fluid nature of decision making in an anecdote about a product crisis:

> The issue was a product defect … how to communicate the defect, especially to Wall
> Street. So a group of us met—the CEO, CFO, marketing VP, legal, manufacturing,
> PR. I left the meeting thinking we'd come to a reasonable decision. But after the meet-
> ing broke up—and I found this out later—the CEO, CFO, and marketing VP met in
> the CEO's office. They then had a teleconference with the head of the manufacturing
> operation where the problem was discovered. Then, the CEO left for a business trip,
> and the CFO traveled with him to the airport. That evening the CEO called the CFO,
> who in turn contacted the lawyer, who was waiting for me in my office the next morn-
> ing to tell me the whole approach had changed. So, while I was part of the central deci-
> sion-making group, at least four other decision-making sessions were held later, and I
> wasn't part of them.

A former public relations executive in an industrial company characterized
shifting venues as "moments" in a "long chain of discussions pertinent to decision
making, and sometimes PR may not even know about some moments, let alone be
in them." The executives suggested two tactics to deal with shifting venues. First,
practitioners who understand organizational decision-making practices might an-
ticipate venue shifts and attempt to insert themselves into the process. Second,
practitioners might try to create informal moments with key decision makers to advocate the role and position of public relations and "stay in the process."

Proposition 3:   The absence of a leading power broker (e.g., CEO, president)
in a meeting of the dominant coalition is a troubling and powerful form of presence.

Without exception, the public relations executives said their company's CEO or
president was the leading member of the dominant coalition, and he or she often was

the key decision maker for significant (and sometimes less significant) issues. Interaction with the top officer is therefore vital. The public relations executives also suggested that the absence of the CEO in key meetings presents other difficulties. The power of the CEO is literally present even when he or she is absent from such meetings in that the group's decisions or recommendations still need to be "run past" the CEO and "blessed." Often, the CEO will ask the president, CFO, or senior legal counselor to provide a briefing subsequent to the key meeting. As a result, this messenger to the CEO holds power to frame and interpret the group's views.

Those interviewed indicated they seldom were asked to play the messenger's role and felt this diluted the weight of their counsel. Two of those interviewed said the CEO in their companies was absent from key meetings so often that they believed it was a strategic move, one leading to "decision making in the shadows." A number of others, however, said this happened infrequently, although it was problematic when it did.

> Proposition 4:   From a public relations perspective, decisions by the dominant coalition are seldom final: There are subsequent check points on public relations power—everywhere.

Given the existence of multiple-dominant coalitions and shifting venues, the decision-making structure in large organizations is somewhat porous; that is, there are multiple points of entry into the process. On one hand this represents opportunities for individuals or functions to participate in decision making. On the other hand, and especially from a public relations perspective, this also means there are numerous checkpoints—for example, editorial reviews and document sign off procedures—on decisions and deliverables that flow out of this structure. Thus, final decisions are not always final, and agreed-on approaches are subject to change. Most public relations executives expressed frustration with this ongoing "tweaking" and "adjustment" process. As one VP of a large energy company put it:

> Everything has to be reviewed: releases, story copy, speeches, Q & As, backgrounders, brochures, everything. And often several times. This leads to changes in texts, of course, and over time the original message or purpose may get tweaked so much you hardly recognize it. I think this is an ongoing political tactic used by others … to press their views through review and approval stages and ultimately affect decisions or texts.

Sometimes original decisions or texts are altered significantly, as Jackall (1988) described in his account of a large container corporation and the production of an environmental report by a public relations agency. The company wanted the agency to produce a study demonstrating that consumers were more interested in economic growth than in environmental protection. The agency did the research and found that consumers did want economic growth but not at the cost of environmental protection. The company was furious when the report reflected these findings. As a result, the agency scurried to produce a series of increasingly blander reports until one less-than-accurate but acceptable report was crafted.

From a public relations perspective, then, various checkpoints following decision making may erode the power of public relations counsel and render somewhat elusive notions of honesty and integrity in communications. As several executives pointed out, however, the checkpoints also can be used by public relations personnel to attempt to counter or modify misleading texts or questionable decisions.

Proposition 5:   The dominant coalition may value the strategic counsel of public relations, but it inevitably demands a set of deliverables (texts) that highlight technical skills.

Spicer (1997) contended that organizational decisions have both instrumental and symbolic functions. The *instrumental* function refers to a concrete action taken, or the result of a decision; the *symbolic* function is the meanings that may be conveyed to publics, or received by publics, through communication or enactment of the decision. A plant closing, for example, is an instrumental function of a decision, but what is communicated about the closing, and how it is communicated, are symbolic functions. Spicer focused on problems that develop when symbolic and instrumental functions of decisions are not complementary.

The public relations executives also spoke to such disconnects, often in the sense of how members of the dominant coalition, following a decision, would then turn their attention to symbolic aspects of the decision, raising such questions as, "What's our public posture going to be?" "How should we position this?" or "How can PR help us convince key publics that this is the right decision?" Interviewees felt these questions separated actual decisions from the public relations or symbolic aspects of them.

The executives also called attention to two products flowing out of dominant coalitions: *decisions*, which translate into actions and values, and *deliverables*, which are usually texts of one form or another that are delivered to, or enacted with, publics. The text deliverables—news releases, speeches, position statements, newsletter copy, announcements—represent symbolic products, and critical discourse analysts see public relations practitioners as "discourse technologists" who shape discourse through the production and dissemination of texts (Fairclough, 1995; Motion & Leitch, 1996).

Although not using this terminology, many public relations executives spoke about text deliverables, linking relationships between decisions and their managerial or strategic role, and text deliverables and their technical roles. Even though the executives are members of dominant coalitions, they often feel more valued for their technical role than for their strategic role. One VP of a financial services company said:

> We argue, negotiate, compromise, advocate in decision making. We wear a strategic hat in these discussions. But once a decision is reached, attention turns to deliverables—our position statements for the press, our speeches to Wall Street. So we put our technical hats back on. Sometimes we're partners in decision making in the eyes of others: *always* we are technicians and wordsmiths, we prepare and deliver messages. You can't escape these roots; they're a big part of your identity, at least in my company.

Proposition 6: Public relations professionals are not immune to pressures of organizational compliance.

A former colleague often spoke of the "golden handcuffs" that organizations attach to those who ascend the ranks. The handcuffs increasingly tighten members to the organization and achievement of its goals. However, the handcuffs are golden in that the organization, in turn, provides generous salaries, excellent benefits, and a position as a power broker. As a result, large corporations are to some degree closed, self-referential environments marked by managerial allegiance to a system where existing culture, rules, historical practices, and power benefits constrain actual or perceived discretionary power (Spicer, 1997). Jackall (1988) suggested that such bureaucratic structures require professionals in any function to be especially attentive to the demands and whims of senior executives. Public relations professionals, he contended, must meet these same bureaucratic demands and "above all satisfy his clients' desires to construct the world in certain ways" (p. 170).

Thus, the pressures of organizational compliance and corresponding material and social benefits that accrue to public relations managers in the dominant coalition may render doing the right thing even more difficult. A handful of public relations executives spoke candidly about these pressures. One VP of a food retail operation said:

> My former boss told me there were two important things about an executive position: the position and what it brought to the individual, and the individual and the experiences, ideas, and values he or she brought to the position. The position gives you power, status, and monetary benefits, which create social status in the company, community, and professional circles. Who doesn't like these things? But my boss said there's always tension between the position and the individual. He was pessimistic because he believed power stays in the position; individuals come and go, but the power stays. So, bottom line, you can't take it with you, so take advantage of it ... and don't mess it up.

Another VP at a chemical company spoke of the ongoing pressures of organizational compliance using an unusual comparison of cowboys and farmers:

Organizations often say they want rugged individuals and people with unique perspectives: you know, cowboys who ride alone, live on the land, and win the gunfights. But what they really want are farmers—folks who mind their own business, tend their land, respect those fence lines. I don't think public relations cowboys make it into the dominant coalition, farmers do. And farmers don't become cowboys once they're there.

There may be studies demonstrating that public relations professionals are more immune than others to the pressures of organizational compliance, but I am not familiar with them. This is not to disparage practitioners or highlight the dark side of practice, as Jackall (1988) had done. Rather, this section critiqued the dominant coalition and through six propositions traced out some of the constraints on public relations managers who seek to do the right thing. These include the presence of multiple coalitions, shifting coalition venues and roles, multiple checkpoints on public relations power through review processes, the separation of instrumental and symbolic functions in decision making, and pressures for organizational compliance.

The extent to which these constraints influence the role and power of public relations may vary based on the expertise, experience, and values of the public relations manager; organizational type, size, culture, and historical practices; and the world views and values of others in dominant coalitions. Nevertheless, the six propositions suggest that doing the right thing is difficult for public relations executives who make it into inner circles. In addition, the role and legitimacy of public relations may be undermined due to another factor that surfaced in the interviews—a gendered dialectic between power relations in inner circles.

RELATIONS OF POWER—A GENDERED DIALECTIC?

Actual public relations practices may grow out of three power relations at play in the dominant coalition. In the power–control perspective, power is located in the interactions between people (Spicer, 1997), and these interactions are referred to here as *power relations*. Power over relations refer to a dominance model, that is, an instrumental and controlling orientation in decision making and discourse. This model is reflected in an asymmetrical world view in the public relations literature (J. E. Grunig, 2001), in several longer theoretical lines (e.g., traditional Marxism and Weberian conflict theory), and in actual capitalist management structures and discourse practices (Deetz, 1992; Weaver, 2001).

Power over relations are today more often conceptualized as "hegemony," a noncoercive form of domination in which "subordinated groups actively consent to and support belief systems and structures of power relations that do not necessarily serve ... those groups' interests" (Mumby, 1997, p. 344). Existing dominance structures and organizational practices and discourses produce a world view that is "acceptable" to both the powerful and the relatively powerless (Deetz & Mumby, 1990). On this view, public relations supports such power relationships through the production of persuasive texts and strategic attempts to influence discourse (Gandy, 1992; Leitch & Neilson, 1997; Weaver, 2001). Juliet Roper (2005/this issue) provides an insightful, in-depth treatment of such hegemonic discourses and practices.

An alternative approach, power with relations, refers to shared power and collaborative decision making (Kanter, 1979; Rakow, 1989). The ideology of shared power highlights the values of interaction, dialogue, cooperation, and relationships rather than power conceptions (Bologh, 1990; L. A. Grunig, Toth, & Hon, 2001; Hartsock, 1981; Rakow, 1989; Shepherd, 1992). Similarly, the two-way symmetrical model of excellent public relations emphasizes shared power with stakeholders that is achieved through dialogue, negotiation, collaboration, and substantive relationship building (J. E. Grunig, 2001).

Bologh (1990) contrasted these power relations in her critique of Max Weber's political realism. Simplifying, she argued that Weber sees the world as a site of ongoing conflicts where actors struggle to impose their will and view on others and where relationships grow out of dominance and coercion. These power over relations represent a distinctly masculine world for Bologh, one that contrasts sharply with her feminist view wherein noncoercive relationships and organizational forms are possible and dialogue, mutual recognition, and empowerment are valorized. Life may be characterized by self interests, coercion, and conflicts, but Bologh contended that life also involves our "responsiveness to and respect for the other" (p. 215) and our essential "rootedness in relationships" (p. 216). Weberian thinking is flawed because it fails to "take an interactive, relational perspective" (p. 288) with others.

If we extend Bologh's (1990) argument to public relations, and substitute business competition for conflict, and business organizations for political or social institutions, then we may identify similar sets of power relations in dominant coalitions in organizations. On one hand, power over relations are manifest when coalition members advocate or support decisions that are self-interested, exclude or restrict other points of view, are nondialogic, and view public relations primarily as an influence variable. On the other hand, power with relations are in play when members advocate or support decisions or decision-making processes that are noncoercive, self-reflective, inclusive of other points of view, and consider public relations to be an important relationship variable.

I suggest there is an ongoing dialectic between these two relations of power, which are not stable, permanently fixed, or necessarily associated with particular individuals or functions. Power over relations are not restricted to the CEO or CFO, for example, and power with relations are not the exclusive province of public relations or human resource managers. Power over relations may characterize decision-making, goals, and resource allocations in many capitalist corporations (Weaver, 2001), but the presence of instrumental power also creates space for power with relations and may stimulate power to relations or forms of resistance.

Thus, as much as public relations practitioners struggle to gain entry into the dominant coalition, once there they are likely enjoined in an intensified dialectic of power relations, which might also be seen as gender loaded. A number of feminist scholars have theoretically and empirically addressed inequities and difficulties women confront in the work place and profession (e.g., L. A. Grunig et al., 2001; Rakow, 1989). Other researchers have suggested that two-way symmetrical public relations approaches are associated with a feminine world view, whereas instrumental orientations in practice may be rooted in male values (Kanter, 1977; J. E. Grunig, 1992; L. A. Grunig, Toth, & Hon, 2000). Drawing from this work and Bologh (1990), I suggest that the dialectic of power relations in the dominant coalition may be a gendered dialectic.

Most members of the dominant coalition in large corporations are men, and it is possible that these men (or even women holding such perspectives) consciously or unconsciously equate two-way symmetrical approaches and shared-power ideology with feminist viewpoints. In the dualism reflected in the dominance perspective—power and powerlessness, winners and losers, strength and weakness, rational and irrational—women represent weakness, irrationality, powerlessness, and emotionality (Bologh, 1990; Rakow, 1989). Does symmetrical public relations, or shared-power ideology, whether advocated by female or male practitioners in the dominant coalition, represent similar "weaknesses" in the eyes of some power brokers?

Most of the executives interviewed suggested that the function is seen as weak and irrational by some power brokers. When asked to describe the types of resistance to shared-power advocacy they encountered in dominant coalitions, the executives identified a handful of cliched perceptions about the profession: Public relations is a soft science—nice to do but of no measurable economic value; inclusive approaches do not make sense in an us-against-them, dog-eat-dog business world; relationships are nice but we are not in the relationship-building business; and emotional responses are detrimental to the bottom line. One public relations director provided this gendered description of power relations in the dominant coalition:

> Sometimes there are multiple camps in these committees, but usually two. One wants to open issues up, get others involved, be more open and candid in communications, while the other is adamantly opposed and thinks such approaches are cop outs, or ways of avoiding tough decisions. I mean, here we are, all married together in these committees, but it's like there's inevitably an impending divorce. The bottom line view of public relations? Hey, can't live with them, can't live without them. What's that sound like!

According to the executives, then, a number of organizational constraints and a gendered dialectic in dominant coalitions curb their abilities to advocate effectively and do the right thing. Some suggested that more education and experience mitigate such constraints (Dozier et al., 1995; L. A. Grunig, J. E. Grunig, Dozier, 2002), and the executives agreed, emphasizing the value of political experience in organizations and the importance of longer term relationships with other members of dominant coalitions. In addition, they spoke to an important third set of relations—what I refer to as power to relations—subsumed in the dialectic in dominant coalitions.

POWER TO RELATIONS—FORMS OF RESISTANCE

Power to relations refer to approaches, processes, and resources that public relations managers (and others) may use to try to counter or resist a dominance model. These political resources, or forms of resistance, may be classified broadly as *sanctioned* and *unsanctioned*. Sanctioned forms of resistance are seen as working "within the system" and are therefore acceptable in the organization. Such approaches are more often presented or described as ways to enhance advocacy and advance the function and role, rather than as forms of resistance. They also may appear to represent pathways toward greater organizational compliance or co-optation of the function (Rakow, 1989). However, these approaches can be characterized as forms of resistance to the extent that they are used to counter a dominance model in the interests of others and not used as approaches to advancing one's career or to carrying out instrumental directives more successfully or efficiently.

Perhaps the most obvious form of sanctioned resistance in public relations is enhanced professional skill—education, knowledge, and experience—that may translate into more effective advocacy of shared-power in the dominant coalition (L. A. Grunig, 1992). Related to this is what Spicer (1997) referred to as the "power of performance" (p. 151), or performing at high levels, documenting and communicating results, and adapting the best practices of other professionals and organizations. Spicer suggested that the power of performance is an increasingly important power base that practitioners can use to "win" in the dominant coalition. A third and established form of resistance is to build alliances with other individuals, groups, and functions. A VP described the formation of such a coalition in her company:

> It started out as an informal group of six women. In the beginning, we mostly shared our frustrations and agreed to work together to help other women and to monitor company actions regarding opportunities for women. Over time, several men joined the group. We had some differences, but we found common ground in that we all believed in more dialogue. So at every opportunity, each of us in our different functions advo-

cated for increased dialogue, more transparency, in decision making. We did this by closely tracking and challenging significant committee memberships and meeting agendas. Several secretaries helped us gain access to agendas and minutes.

A fourth form of sanctioned resistance is to construct highly rational arguments based on substantive evidence, that is, to develop data-based claims of superior weight. Because corporations often use an economic calculus in decision making, public relations managers also can legitimate claims by using such calculations. One reading of current intensive research into relationship and reputation measurement is that such attempts seek to document the economic advantages of two-way symmetrical public relations and relationship building in a rational manner that "fits" the economic calculus utilized in the dominant coalition. One public relations director at a consumer electronics firm provided an interesting corollary to this approach:

> It took me a long time to learn the value of advocating the risks of *not* doing something. So much of the time, and we are taught to do this, our plans highlight the benefits of doing something, or the need to do something. But in several board meetings I attended, it seemed the CEO mostly described the dangers inherent in not doing something. I began to use this type of fear appeal with some success. At least it captures attention.

An encompassing fifth form of sanctioned resistance refers to enhancing political astuteness or becoming a more effective player in the political infrastructure of the organization. Drawing from interviews with public relations practitioners, Spicer (1997) characterized the politically astute organizational member in this way:

> The politically astute organizational member has knowledge of the formal and informal decision-making process: He or she knows how to use the system to his or her advantage. Knowledge of the process of decision-making is grounded in being able to identify the key players and knowing their strengths, weaknesses, penchants, hidden agendas, personal likes and dislikes, and their degree of political astuteness. Political astuteness demands that one be aware of human nature, of the strengths and weaknesses of those with whom one interacts. (p. 145)

If political astuteness is important, then public relations educational approaches bear examination. Current undergraduate programs focus on mastering technical competencies but pay little attention to organizational politics or political astuteness. We could benefit from case studies and seminars that provide greater insights into political dimensions of the job, and Spicer's (1997) text is a good starting point. Knowing what public relations managers should accomplish in the dominant coalition is important; knowing how to do so is no less significant.

Unsanctioned Resistance

Unsanctioned forms of resistance refer to actions or approaches that are "outside the system" and unacceptable to the organization. For practitioners these more radical forms of activism may challenge allegiance to the organization, represent real career threats, and pose difficult ethical dilemmas. We know little about unsanctioned resistance in the profession and associated issues and dilemmas. Identifying various forms of radical activism, however, may raise awareness and increase dialogue about such issues and their implications. Four broad categories of unsanctioned forms of resistance are briefly detailed here: covert actions, alternative interpretations, whistleblowing, and association-level activism.

Leaks and counterculture actions may be the most common forms of covert resistance. Leaks refer to the delivery of sensitive information to key outside parties, for example, reporter or government official. I am not referring to proprietary information such as product specifications, patent data, or strategic marketing information so much as to information that corrects or contradicts "misleading" information that is directed for official release. One retired public relations VP, for example, described how information was deliberately leaked to a local reporter regarding a company media program touting career opportunities for minorities:

> I didn't support the program because I felt it was a false campaign, another fashionable program of the month. So I gave some data to a reporter I'd known for a long time and encouraged him to contact an EEO official for more information. I'm embarrassed to say I did this through pay phones, real cloak-and-dagger stuff. The upshot was a critical story appeared, the company scaled back the program, but did hire two minority candidates. I can't say I'm proud of what I did, but I felt good about it. Does that make sense?

Counterculture actions come in various forms but often involve initiating communications and formulating interpretations that oppose those in formal communications. Several VPs mentioned that the grapevine was not only a source of rumors and information but also an outlet for planting rumors and information. One VP described a situation in which the local dominant coalition decided to formally position the loss of a major business contract as a product quality problem for which operational employees were responsible:

> The reality was, we lost the business because we took too long to respond to a customer bid. It wasn't a product quality issue at all—it was a decision-making problem. But my protests were overruled and I was given my directives, which I carried out. But I also shared the real story with a friend in production, who spread the rumor on the grapevine, and someone, maybe him, posted anonymous memos with the story on bulletin boards. Within 24 hours management was retreating, and the incident became an important marker in future communication decisions.

Groups often construct their own interpretations of formal communications and actions. Many of the public relations executives indicated they were usually candid with their employees and peers in reporting developments in dominant coalitions and in providing alternative interpretations. Creating and sharing alternate interpretations may be a common form of resistance. It is unsanctioned in that one tacit rule governing those in the dominant coalition is that members are expected to mouth the party line, even if they disagree with it. This represents team playing at high levels. One VP in a manufacturing company said:

> Championing a bad party line has always been difficult for me, especially with my own people. When they ask me what really happened in some meeting, or why the company made such-and-such a decision, I tell them flat out. We discuss the issue and what it really means and develop some common understanding. And then they go out and share this interpretation with their friends in the company, who tell others. The irony is, we do this even as we carry out the approved communication activities.

This comment resonates with Mumby's (1997) reading of Scott's (1990) discussion of subordinate groups' resistance to hegemony, wherein groups use low-profile resistance practices to construct interpretations and shared meanings that run counter to the dominant discourse. Like the public relations group previously, "subordinate groups can outwardly or denotatively express acquiescence to the prevailing order, while simultaneously and connotatively defying it" (p. 363). One wonders if practitioners, highly competent in crafting dominant corporate discourses, might be equally capable of constructing dissident discourses.

Whistleblowing, or reporting legal or ethical violators, can occur internally or externally. All of the executives interviewed indicated their companies had ethical codes and mechanisms for reporting violators, but few could recall actual use or enforcement of such codes. None of the executives interviewed had used this form of resistance, and they felt it was little used by other public relations practitioners for reasons highlighted in this comment by one VP:

> I can't visualize PR people doing that. I mean, look at the PRSA code of ethics. It's been around for decades, but what have there been, maybe 50 violations reported? If we don't snitch on professionals who are doing something wrong, I can't imagine we would report our own executives. Ratting people out just isn't very acceptable in most contexts.

Association-level activism represents another potential form of resistance, though there is little evidence that the Public Relations Society of America (PRSA), International Association of Business Communicators, or similar organizations have carried out or are interested in activist approaches, given their penchant for skills development to improve practitioners' service to executives and organizations. What might such associations do to advocate power with relations and resist a dominance model? Small steps might include devoting conference sessions to political astuteness, preparing case studies of public relations and power issues inside the dominant coalition, and establishing working groups to address such topics.

More radical forms of association activism might include issuing statements or staging demonstrations to protest deplorable corporate or public relations practices, for example, handling of the Exxon Valdez case or the more recent frauds perpetrated by officials at Enron, WorldCom, and other corporations. Why has PRSA not taken a sharper stand on these recent developments? At the least, public relations managers in these companies were unknowingly complicit in constructing corporate images and discourses that were at odds with underlying practices and ethics. With the integrity and reputation of executives and corporations under fire on many fronts today, there may be no better time for practitioners and academics to mobilize and press their organizations for greater social accountability and transparency. Such activism might help legitimate the profession, provide a mechanism for organizational learning and self-reflection, and more closely align private–public values and norms (Jensen, 2001).

DISCUSSION

Symmetrical public relations theory emphasizes a relational orientation characterized by dialogue, compromise, and shared power. This normative framework represents doing the right thing in practice but, perhaps caught up in its own relational logic, neglects power considerations that influence practice (Cheney & Christensen, 2001). Although theorists acknowledge the dominant coalition as a locus of organizational power, they have revealed little of the dynamic power relations at play in this inner circle. As a result, there are gaps in the literature between what ought to be done, what prevents it from getting done, and how it might get done.

This article has reflected on these gaps. My critique of the dominant coalition, formulated in six propositions, surfaced a matrix of constraints on practitioners. I then described a dialectic between power over and power with relations in the dominant coalition and suggested this dialectic is gender loaded. If this is so—and the idea was not fully developed here—public relations advocacy of shared power is likely to be equated with a feminine ideology and therefore dismissed by some power brokers as ineffectual in a "world seen to require" a masculine ideology and corresponding relations of dominance rather than mutuality or cooperation. Finally, I outlined some forms of resistance that practitioners might use to try to mitigate some of these constraints and strengthen power to relations.

My critique bears at least two implications for theory and practice. First, any public relations theory is deficient to the extent it fails to account for power relations and structures in organizations. This is not a new claim but rather one further legitimated here through in-depth interviews with 21 public relations executives. Power is not something "out there" beyond the practice but instead constitutive of practice in shifting relations of power that both constrain and create opportunities for choices and actions. As the executives indicated, power ebbs and flows and moves through various venues and moments of decision making so that practice seems inevitably bound up in relations of power. If we are to illuminate public relations practice and elaborate its possibilities we need more sophisticated theories that incorporate power relations and their manifold influences on public relations practitioners, practices, and strategies. The six propositions presented in this article may be used as hypotheses for testing in this regard.

Second, to more fully understand the pressures on and performance of public relations professionals, it also seems necessary to consider the group, organizational, and social contexts of practice as well as the professional background and orientation of the practitioner. Judy Motion and C. Kay Weaver (2005/this issue) provide a substantive analysis of the political, economic and social contexts of public relations practices and discourses in their case study of Life Sciences Network. They argue that understanding such contexts is essential to analyzing and theorizing the practice.

I have focused on the dominant coalition as a central decision-making group in the organization but paid scant attention to the social contexts of practice or the orientations and values of individual practitioners. Although the public relations executives identified a number of very real structural and power relations problems they confront on the job, this web of constraints is nevertheless only one level of complexity that should not mask a deeper and perhaps more fundamental level of complexity, that is, the essential dissonance in the practice itself. Whom do practitioners serve? Their own career interests? The organization? The profession? The interests of others in the margins? The larger society? Moreover, who is defining that service (Rakow, 1989)? Is it the practitioner? The professional association? The CEO or other top manager? A journalist or community official outside the organization?

These conflicting interests and perspectives create tension in practitioners and highlight the importance of roles taken on in practice, which cannot be separated from whom or what one serves or how one is defined. Those serving their own interests will adopt roles that best accommodate achievement of self-interests. Those who serve the organization and achievement of its financial and market objectives are likely to take on roles wherein they carry out instrumental directives as efficiently and effectively as possible. Those who seek to serve the interests of the organization and greater society are likely to find their roles to be complex and constrained. Diverse definitions of roles and interests, found even among professionals working in the same public relations team or function, render even more difficult the determination of what public relations will be and how it will be used in an organization.

Currently the literature characterizes or defines two roles for public relations professionals: technician and manager. However, limiting our practice field to these two roles may have defined us into a conundrum. Technicians play an important production role but this credential is insufficient to gain admission to the dominant coalition. Managers possess stronger professional portfolios that increase the likelihood of admission. However, there is no guarantee that managers who make it into inner circles will either be able to or want to do the "right" thing. Some will find themselves seriously constrained in their attempts due to existing power relations and organizational structures and practices. Others may be perfectly content inside the inner circle to serve only themselves or their organizations.

Such complexities suggest that it is time to consider a third role for public relations professionals—that of activist. This role grows out of power to relations, or forms of resistance to a dominance model. In the activist role, a practitioner must go beyond advocacy of doing the right thing to carrying out actions to support and supplement advocacy in the organization and larger social system. This article has sketched out a few forms of activism and resistance, but a great deal more research is necessary to clarify a repertoire of sanctioned and unsanctioned forms of resistance and to examine in depth the significant ethical questions and practice implications that accompany this role and these forms of resistance.

One area of opportunity may lie in greater activism on a national level through the combined efforts of thousands of practitioners, teachers, and students who constitute a potentially large and influential activist community. Through new agendas in current associations, or more likely through formation of alternative coalitions, members might combine advocacy of shared power with activism in the interest of shared power. Here we can learn from and use some of the tactics of social movement groups, for example, routinely providing an activist perspective on current events to media outlets; advocating directly or indirectly with organizational leaders through letters, advertisements, or alternative Web sites; or staging special events to garner attention. Can we imagine 1,000 or 10,000 public relations practitioners and academics marching, demonstrating, and lobbying enthusiastically—in the glare of media spotlights—in the interests of shared power and greater organizational transparency?

Although it may be difficult to hold this image, can we nevertheless not envision the possibility sketched out by Frank Durham (2005/this issue) of public relations professionals playing the role of "potentially powerful social actors" rather than, or in addition to, the roles of technicians and managers who help maintain and are simultaneously constrained by the organizations they serve? Furthermore, if doing the right thing in public relations is important, and if symmetrical public relations is itself not simply a hegemonic discourse, then before we comply with the status quo or dismiss the possibility as foolishly idealistic are we not obligated as professionals, teachers, and researchers to take up some forms of resistance that will move us forward from claims and advocacy in our relatively obscure journals and trade publications to more engaged activism in the public world?

At the least, contemplating an activist role for public relations will force us to render more transparent the realities of power relations in dominant coalitions and other organizational structures and processes that touch the practice from virtually every side, at every turn. Acknowledging the power that organizations hold over public relations practices and possibilities, as well as the pressures for conformity and complicity in the exercise of this power, seems an important step on the way to opening up and realizing alternative public relations conceptions and possibilities (Rakow, 1989).

An activist public relations role also might begin to subtly alter relations of power inside dominant coalitions as well as influence perceptions of the practice in the general public. Although some forms of resistance may seem modest, or even futile, it is important to remember that the choices and actions of those who challenge prevailing power structures do influence those structures and relations of power, even as they are influenced by them (Conrad, 1983; Giddens, 1979; Lukes, 1974). If definitions of issues and roles help define power relations, as Stone (1988) suggested, then changing definitions of the roles of public relations may help move us along the path toward changing power relations and doing the "right" thing.

REFERENCES

Allen, T. J. (1979). *Managing the flow of technology: Technology transfer and the dissemination of technological information with the research and development organization.* Cambridge, MA: MIT Press.

Bachrach, S., & Lawler, E. (1980). *Power and politics in organizations.* San Francisco: Jossey-Bass.

Bologh, R. W. (1990). *Love or greatness: Max Weber and masculine thinking—A feminist inquiry.* London: Unwin Hyman.

Broom, G. M., & Dozier, D. M. (1985, August). *Determinants and consequences of public relations roles.* Paper presented at the meeting of the Association for Education in Journalism and Mass Communication, Memphis, TN.

Broom, G. M., & Dozier, D. M. (1986). Advancement for public relations role models. *Public Relations Review, 12,* 37–56.

Burger, D. (1983). How management views public relations. *Public Relations Quarterly, 27*(4), 27–30.

Cheney, G., & Christensen, L. T. (2001). Public relations as contested terrain: A critical response. In R. L. Heath (Ed.), *Handbook of public relations* (pp. 167–182). Thousand Oaks, CA: Sage.

Child, J. (1972). Organizational structure, environment, and performance: The role of strategic choice. *Sociology, 6*(1), 2–22.

Conrad, C. (1983). Organizational power: Faces and symbolic form. In L. L. Putnam & M. E. Pacanowsky (Eds.), *Communications and organizations: An interpretive approach* (pp. 173–194). Beverly Hills, CA: Sage.

Cyert, R. M., & March, J. G. (1963). *A behavioral theory of the firm.* Englewood Cliffs, NJ: Prentice-Hall.

Daugherty, E. L. (2001). Public relations and social responsibility. In R. L. Heath (Ed.), *Handbook of public relations* (pp. 389–402). Thousand Oaks, CA: Sage.

Deetz, S. A. (1992). *Democracy in the age of corporate colonization: Developments in communication and the politics of everyday life.* Albany: State University of New York Press.

Deetz, S. A., & Mumby, D. K. (1990). Power, discourse, and the workplace: Reclaiming the critical tradition. In J. Anderson (Ed.), *Communication yearbook 13* (pp. 18–47). Newbury Park, CA: Sage.

Dozier, D. M. (1983, November). *Toward a reconciliation of "role conflict" in public relations research.* Paper presented at the meeting of the Western communications educators conference, Fullerton, CA.

Dozier, D. M. (1984). Program evaluation and roles of practitioners. *Public Relations Review, 10*(2), 13–21.

Dozier, D. M. (1992). The organizational roles of communication and public relations practitioners. In J. E. Grunig (Ed.), *Excellence in public relations and communication management* (pp. 327–355). Hillsdale, NJ: Lawrence Erlbaum Associates, Inc.

Dozier, D. M., Grunig, L. A., & Grunig, J. E. (1995). *Manager's guide to excellence in public relations and communication management.* Mahwah, NJ: Lawrence Erlbaum Associates, Inc.

Durham, F. (2005/this issue). Public relations as structuration: A prescriptive critique of the StarLink global food contamination case. *Journal of Public Relations Research, 17,* 29–47.

Ehling, W. P. (1992). Public relations education and professionalism. In J. E. Grunig (Ed.), *Excellence in public relations and communication management* (pp. 439–466). Hillsdale, NJ: Lawrence Erlbaum Associates, Inc.

Fairclough, N. (1995). *Critical discourse analysis.* New York: Longman.

French, J. R. P., & Raven, B. (1959). The bases of social power. In D. Cartwright (Ed.), *Studies in social power* (pp. 150–167). Ann Arbor: University of Michigan Institute for Social Research.

Gandy, O. (1992). Public relations and public policy: The structuration of dominance in the information age. In E. Toth & R. Heath (Eds.), *Rhetorical and critical approaches to public relations* (pp. 131–164). Hillsdale, NJ: Lawrence Erlbaum Associates, Inc.

Giddens, A. (1979). *Central problems in social theory: Action, structure and contradiction in social analysis.* Berkeley: University of California Press.

Gossen, R., & Sharp, K. (1987). Workshop: How to manage dispute resolution. *Public Relations Journal, 43*(12), 35–37.

Grunig, J. E. (Ed.). (1992). *Excellence in public relations and communications management.* Hillsdale, NJ: Lawrence Erlbaum Associates, Inc.

Grunig, J. E. (2001). Two-way symmetrical public relations: Past, present and future. In R. L. Heath (Ed.), *Handbook of public relations* (pp. 11–30). Thousand Oaks, CA: Sage.

Grunig, J. E., & Grunig, L. A. (1989). Toward a theory of the public relations behavior of organizations: Review of a program of research. In J. E. Grunig & L. A. Grunig (Eds.), *Public relations research annual* (Vol. 1, pp. 27–63). Hillsdale, NJ: Lawrence Erlbaum Associates, Inc.

Grunig, J. E., & Grunig, L. A. (1992). Models of public relations and communication. In J. E. Grunig (Ed.), *Excellence in public relations and communication management* (pp. 285–325). Hillsdale, NJ: Lawrence Erlbaum Associates, Inc.

Grunig, J. E., & Hunt, T. (1984). *Managing public relations.* New York: Holt, Rinehart & Winston.

Grunig, L. A. (1992). Power in the public relations department. In J. E. Grunig (Ed.), *Excellence in public relations and communications management* (pp. 483–501). Hillsdale, NJ: Lawrence Erlbaum Associates, Inc.

Grunig, L. A., Grunig, J. E., & Dozier, D. M. (2002). *Excellent public relations and effective organizations*. Mahwah, NJ: Lawrence Erlbaum Associates, Inc.

Grunig, L. A., Toth, E. L., & Hon, L. C. (2000). Feminist values in public relations. *Journal of Public Relations Research, 12*(1), 49–68.

Grunig, L. A., Toth, E. L., & Hon, L. C. (2001). *Women in public relations: How gender influences practice*. New York: Guilford.

Hage, J. (1980). *Theories of organizations: Form, process, and transformation*. New York: Wiley.

Hartsock, N. (1981). Political change: Two perspectives on power. In Quest Staff and Book Committee (Eds.), *Building feminist theory* (pp. 3–19). New York: Longman.

Jackall, R. (1988). *Moral mazes: The world of corporate managers*. New York: Oxford University Press.

Jensen, I. (2001). Public relations and emerging functions of the public sphere: An analytical framework. *Journal of Communication Management, 6,* 133–147.

Kanter, R. M. (1977). *Men and women of the corporation*. New York: Basic Books.

Kanter, R. M. (1979, July–August). Power failure in management circuits. *Harvard Business Review*, pp. 65–75.

Lauzen, M. M., & Dozier, D. M. (1992). The missing link: The public relations manager role as mediator of organizational environments and power consequences for the function. *Journal of Public Relations Research, 4,* 205–220.

Leitch, S., & Neilson, D. (1997). Reframing public relations: New directions for theory and practice. *Australian Journal of Communication, 24*(2), 17–32.

Lukes, S. (1974). *Power: A radical view*. London: Macmillan.

Mintzberg, H. (1983). *Power in and around organizations*. Englewood Cliffs, NJ: Prentice-Hall.

Motion, J., & Leitch, S. (1996). A discursive perspective from New Zealand: Another world view. *Public Relations Review, 22,* 297–309.

Motion, J., & Weaver, C. K. (2005/this issue). The discourse perspective for critical public relations research: Life sciences network and the battle for "truth." *Journal of Public Relations Research, 17,* 49–67.

Mumby, D. K. (1997, Fall). The problem of hegemony: Rereading Gramsci for organizational communication studies. *Western Journal of Communication, 61,* 343–375.

Pfeffer, J. (1981) *Power in organizations*. Marshfield, MA: Pitnam.

Plowman, K. D. (1998). Power in conflict for public relations. *Journal of Public Relations Research, 10,* 237–261.

Rakow, L. (1989). From the feminization of public relations to the promise of feminism. In E. L. Toth & C. G. Cline (Eds.), *Beyond the velvet ghetto* (pp. 287–298). San Francisco: IABC Research Foundation.

Roloff, M. E. (1987). Communication and conflict. In C. R. Berger & S. H. Chaffee (Eds.), *The handbook of communication science* (pp. 484–530). Newbury Park, CA: Sage.

Roper, J. (2005/this issue). Symmetrical communication: Excellent public relations or a strategy for hegemony? *Journal of Public Relations Research, 17,* 69–86.

Schneider (a.k.a. Grunig), L. A. (1985). The role of public relations in four organizational types. *Journalism Quarterly, 62,* 567–576, 594.

Scott, J. C. (1990). *Domination and the arts of resistance: Hidden transcripts*. New Haven, CT: Yale University Press.

Shepherd, G. J. (1992). Communication as influence: Definitional exclusion. *Communication Studies, 43,* 203–219.

Simon, H. A. (1976). *Administrative behavior* (3rd ed.). New York: Free Press.

Spicer, C. (1997). *Organizational public relations: A political perspective*. Mahwah, NJ: Lawrence Erlbaum Associates, Inc.

Stone, D. (1988). *Policy paradox and political reason*. New York: HarperCollins.

Strenski, J. B. (1980). The top 12 public relations challenges for 1980. *Public Relations Journal, 36,* 11–14.

Thompson, J. D. (1967). *Organizations in action*. New York: McGraw-Hill.

Weaver, D. K. (2001). Dressing for battle in the new global economy: Putting power, identity, and discourse into public relations theory. *Management Communication Quarterly, 15,* 279–288.

JOURNAL OF PUBLIC RELATIONS RESEARCH, *17*(1), 29–47

Public Relations As Structuration: A Prescriptive Critique of the StarLink Global Food Contamination Case

Frank Durham

School of Journalism and Mass Communication
University of Iowa

In this case study, the contamination of the world food supply with genetically modified (GM) corn in 2000 by the transnational corporation, Aventis CropScience, provides the context for considering how theory and practice can be adapted to support a more dialogue-based approach to public relations. As a poststructural alternative, Giddens's theory of structuration is presented as a paradigmatic alternative to the traditional functionalism that is evident in the Aventis public relations experience.

Genetic engineering was already big business when StarLink hybrid corn contaminated the world food supply in 2000.[1] The resulting crisis proved costly for all concerned, causing multiple lawsuits and staggering financial losses. Within 2 years, the crisis had led to the sale of the beleaguered CropScience division by StarLink's Franco-German producer, the Aventis CropScience corporation.

In this discussion, understanding this crisis means interpreting the actions of the company to theorize a solution for present limitations on the practice of public relations. Based on the normative assumption that corporations would benefit from sharing a mutually adaptable social context with the publics they engage through public relations, this article presents sociologist Anthony Giddens's (1984) theory of structuration as an interpretive alternative to the functionalist paradigm represented by traditional public relations theory and idealized in the concepts of "sym-

---

Requests for reprints should be sent to Frank Durham, School of Journalism and Mass Communication, University of Iowa, 615 Seashore Hall W, Iowa City, IA 52242–1401. Email: frank-durham@uiowa.edu

[1]By 1999, genetically modified crops already represented 25% of U.S. agricultural crops, "including 35 percent of corn, 55 percent of soybeans, and almost half of all cotton" (Blakeslee, 2001, p. 6.)

metry" and "asymmetry" (J. E. Grunig & Hunt, 1984). Following a brief overview of the case, the theory of structuration is explained as it might apply to practice.

As Aventis CropScience sought to introduce StarLink in 1999, the sale of corn was the province of the company's marketing professionals. However selling the *idea* of genetically modified (GM) corn to various publics defined the communications challenge before Aventis CropScience's corporate public relations staff.[2] As discussed in the following case analysis, the crisis reflected an ideological conflict between the company and various publics over the legitimacy of bioengineered food.

Among the dimensions of the crisis—including regulatory conflicts, food contamination, and lawsuits—the top-down role of Aventis's public relations approach was central to the resulting debacle as its communication practices exacerbated this problem. Because of a lack of clear communication to farmers to segregate the transgenic StarLink from ordinary crops, more than 2,000 farmers in 29 states planted the GM corn too close to neighbors' fields, presenting a cross-pollination contamination threat (Hauben, 2000). The company's outreach in response to the crisis was equally static. At a practical level, a larger problem emerged after the corn was harvested, when StarLink corn was mixed with normal corn at a Texas grain mill, contaminating the global food supply (Kaufman, 2000).

Based on this example, this article takes the position that public relations could—and should—proceed in a more dialogue-based fashion predicated on a professional sense of agency. The following discussion centers on a critique of how power is theorized and practiced in corporate public relations today, what that means, and how public relations could be more meaningfully practiced. This question remains more relevant than ever today, as shown in Bruce Berger's (2005/this issue) critique of the "dominant coalition" in public relations and its implicit asymmetries of power. The following discussion presents a similar critique and prescription by explicating the theory of structuration as a way for public relations managers to reposition themselves in a more action-oriented stance within otherwise traditionally institutional contexts.

THEORY

Recent attempts in critical (Berger, 1999; Dozier & Lauzen, 2000; Karlberg, 1996) and postmodern (Holtzhausen, 2000; Holtzhausen & Voto, 2002; Mickey, 1997) public relations scholarship to address the importance of "symmetry" highlight two points: that the notion of "symmetrical" communication is an ideal, and that a consensus exists that the functionalism of mainstream public relations theory needs basic reconsideration. Juliet Roper's (2005/this issue) criti-

---

[2]This definition of public relations corresponds to the model of "social marketing" developed by Kotler (1982) and Kotler and Roberto (1989).

cal article exposes the embedded paradox of power and "symmetry" as she iden-
tifies it as the basis of hegemonic power imbalances. Working in different terms
but from the same premise, this article also asserts that the reified and
oppositional notions of power balance, for example, internal versus external
publics, that underlie traditional notions of "symmetry" undermine public relations communication (J. E. Grunig & Hunt, 1984).

To effect this paradigm shift—which seems universally called for and variously
approached, as the diversity of this theme issue demonstrates—I developed the
interpretivist ontology of Anthony Giddens's (1984) theory of structuration for application to practice. It offers a concept of "dialogue" to public relations practice
that is grounded in multiple perspectives based on independent actors—individual
or collective—their meanings, and the actions they may take to effect change
(Miller, 2000).

Change—with public relations as its corporate agent—becomes more visible
when ideas are new. Both here and in the article by Judy Motion and C. Kay
Weaver (2005/this issue), the advent of genetic engineering presents an opportunity to interpret the often implicit practice of public relations by observing the public process of propagating this new idea as a product. In their discussion of critical
discourse analysis in this essay, Motion and Weaver locate public relations in the
same place, theorizing public relations "as a legitimate tactic in the struggle for
and negotiation of *power*" (p. 50). The question is how to theorize public relations
as a way for corporations to participate in the social processes they otherwise pre-
sume to dominate?

The Theory of Structuration

As a critique of structural functionalism and the production of power, Giddens's
(1984) theory reconceptualized "structure." Where the term *structure* often indicates the functionalist assumption of the permanence, if not just dominance, of
institutional power, in Giddens's work "structuration" made the institution a part
of a fluid process of social production and reproduction. Specifically, the theory
of structuration assumes the susceptibility of the institution to change. As
Mouzelis (1989) explained,

> Structure in Giddens' theory … is both medium and outcome of the conduct it recur-
> sively organizes—a medium because through its use social conduct is produced, and
> an outcome because it is through the production of this conduct that rules and re-
> sources are reproduced in time and space. (p. 615)

Because of the perspective it can offer on institutions and their public relations
practices, Giddens's theory of structuration provided the central analytical basis
for this essay, especially because it allows for the interpretation of power rela-

tions in conflict within more fluid terms than other, traditionally critical theories might describe (Gitlin, 1980; Gramsci, 1971; Williams, 1977, 1980). By characterizing the sociology of such conflicts as social reproduction, Giddens's (1976) theory made it possible to consider the dynamic within which social change takes place:

> To study the structuration of a social system is to study the ways in which that system, via application of generative rules and resources, and in the context of unintended outcomes, is produced and reproduced in interaction ... . [So structuration refers to] the conditions governing the continuity or transformation of structures and, therefore, the reproduction of systems (p. 66)

In this rejection of functionalism, structuration reflects a change from the ostensibly predictable outcomes of strategic action to the assumption that all outcomes must be interpreted as they are produced. Also referred to as "structuring moments," such outcomes are often the events where–and from which—social process is reproduced (Giddens, 1984; Sewell, 1992).

Agency, Action, Power

In defining the theory of structuration as a "theory of action," Giddens (1984) grounded the concept of "action" in practical terms. Instead of referring to individuals' "intentions," he emphasized "their capability of doing things in the first place." As he continued, he emphasized that "agency implies *power* [italics added]: cf. the Oxford English Dictionary definition of an agent, as 'one who exerts power or produces an effect.'" In this sense, taking action becomes a practical option, but not a determined outcome, of an individual's participation in a given social routine. Giddens explained that, "Agency concerns events of which an individual is the perpetrator, in the sense that the individual could, at any phase in a given sequence, have acted differently" (p. 9). The theory suggested that all actors—here, public relations professionals, their institutions, and all other social actors—are implicated in the process of structuration, whether in potential or active ways.

Where "agency" represents the capacity for action, realizing change hinges on whether social actors *will* be aware of their potential within otherwise routine circumstances. Addressing this liminal quality of action as an access-point to social power—whether consciousness will lead to action or not—Giddens (1984) described the ability to be conscious in this way as "reflexivity" or as "the monitored character of the ongoing flow of social life" (p. 3). He described the method for treating agency across levels from the cognitive or subconscious to the interpersonal and socially constructive in terms of its moving from the latent to the active:

"What I call the stratification model of the acting self involves treating the reflex-ive monitoring, rationalization, and motivation of action as embedded sets of pro-cesses" (pp. 3). In those terms, although the premise of the theory of structuration is that individual and collective action can be important parts of the process of re-producing society, the difficulty in taking action stems from the "embedded-"ness of social routines.

According to Giddens (1984), these social patterns created a "mutual knowl-edge," which "is not directly accessible to the consciousness of actors" (p. 4). In-stead, he described the "rationalization of action," as a way to account for the continuities in social routines that mitigate active change. He explained, "I mean that actors—routinely and for the most part without fuss—maintain a continuing 'theoretical understanding' of the grounds of their activity" (p. 5). In the present discussion, the opportunity for public relations practitioners is to become con-scious of their ability to act for change, alone and together, apart from the working routine. Principally, this means taking into account that the corporate workplace and its actions are connected to the world beyond the company walls.

To effect such a change, the first task is to reassess the meaning of one's more or less powerful position within social interactions. Although power—in public re-lations and elsewhere—will be necessarily imbalanced, it is essential that public relations practitioners see that all parties are affected by any interaction. In that sense, Giddens's (1984) approach called for practitioners to set aside the top-down rationalism of their institutional perspectives in favor of locating themselves more reflexively within a holistic perspective. This distinction between reifying the in-stitution as a discrete participant in communication, rather than as an integral part of the whole, is key. Although various paradigms treat social phenomena as dis-crete categories, Weaver and Goia (1994) proposed that Giddens's (1976, 1979, 1984) theory of structuration "provides a means of understanding this selective bracketing and provides a point of connection between the assumptions of interpretivists and functionalists" (as cited in Miller, 2000). They explained that:

> Structuration provides a basis for seeing how ... [we] ... can invoke different assump-tions, pursue different goals, ask different research questions, and use different ap-proaches, but nonetheless be engaged in inquiry with commonalities despite such di-versities ... . Structuration theory shows just how selective bracketing of social phenomena can occur. (Weaver & Goia, 1994, pp. 577–578)

For scholars, structuration theory can serve as a "metatheoretical bridge" be-tween and among postpositivist, critical and interpretivist perspectives (Miller, 2000). For professionals, applying structuration theory to public relations prac-tice would make it possible to reconceptualize corporate institutions as integral parts of ideologically complex contexts. In effect, the benefit comes from being able to interpret cultural diversity as the basis of practice.

Toward a New Public Relations:
Communicating Within the Structured Totality

In traditional terms, public relations practice often helps institutions to defend governing "principles" of social organization, that is, that institutions should act as quasipermanent arbiters of more malleable social "rules."[3] In Giddens's (1979) terms, the typical, collective position of corporations as defenders of normative cultural values makes them representatives of the "most deeply layered practices constitutive of social systems ... *institutions*" (Giddens, 1979, p. 65). By contrast with the idea of structuration, the illusion of functionalism is one of maintaining the status quo, as if change were not endemic and unavoidable (Baumann, 1992).

To accomplish this move toward a more integrated social theory, Giddens (1984) departed from traditional sociologies. Instead, he addressed his theory of structuration to the problems left by the functionalism of Parsons (1949), the structuralism of Althusser (1965, 1971) and Blau (1977), the phenomonology of Schutz (1972), the symbolic interactionism of Goffman (1959), and the ethnomethodology of Garfinkel (1967). According to Baber (1991), Giddens's work "is intended to compensate for the lack of an adequate theory of action" (p. 221) among these exemplars. For Giddens (1984),

> The differences between these perspectives on social science have often been taken to be epistemological, whereas they are, in fact, ontological ... . The basic domain of study of the social sciences, according to the theory of structuration, is neither the experience of the individual actor, nor the experience of any form of social totality, but social practices ordered across space and time. (p. 2)

He explained that "a social system is a 'structured totality.' Structures do not exist in time-space, except in the moments of the constitution of social systems" (Giddens, 1979, pp. 64–65).

By theorizing the combined effect of top-down and bottom-up social interactions in this way, Giddens (1984) offered the concept of the "duality of structure" (pp. 15–16). By describing the concept of "rules and resources," for example, Giddens outlined the flaw in this logic. According to this concept, less powerful social actors can use social rules intended to limit them as targets for action, in effect turning limitations into resources.

Unlike the rationalized binarism of the traditional concept of "symmetry," the effect of Giddens's (1984) "duality" is that institutions are reflexive participants in the contexts they would otherwise govern. Rather than being defined as distinct

---

[3]A key social principle among modern institutions is that they should persist at a level that ensures their dominance, even as they might oversee rules changes that they had previously resisted (Durham, 2002).

parts of a power imbalance, institutions and those they would affect are bound to each other within a common social context. According to Baber (1991), this "*duality of structure* ... implies the transcendence of the structure–agency dichotomy. Structure represents the rules and resources, and exists only in the constituting moments of social systems" (pp. 223–224; see also Sewell, 1992).

For public relations practitioners, the dual nature of conflicts offers both a threat to such institutional stasis and a way to treat it as a venue for change. As he challenged the notion of structure as a fixed set of socially defining principles, Giddens's goal was to account for all participants within a process of social change. Instead of discussing reified social concepts, such as, "target," "internal," or "external" publics, or even "reactive versus proactive" strategies, public relations practitioners should reconsider the implications their presumptive positions within any institutionally "managed" relationship.

In addition, this concept of structuration makes it possible to propose to public relations practitioners that dialogues of change and conflict are valid contexts of social reproduction, offering possibilities that remain invisible to the functionalist eye. Philosophically, this presents a new way of understanding public relations practitioners as potentially powerful social actors, rather than as actors maintaining—and limited by—a rationalized system. As discussed both in this theoretical framework and in the following case analysis, the goal of this essay is to show that public relations practitioners might more consciously and effectively engage the meaningful contexts within which they are working.

METHOD

To identify news stories as data for textual analysis, I searched the "news" section within the "Academic Universe" part of Lexis–Nexis from September 1999 to March 2002 for the terms, *StarLink* and *CropScience*. This search produced 281 articles, including wire service stories that were carried more than once on the same day or within the same period, and stories mentioning the keywords StarLink or CropScience without direct relation to the developing story. I also searched the same terms in the Alt.Press Watch database,[4] where I found 6 articles from nonmainstream newspapers and referred to two.[5] After comparing these articles, I selected 56 as a frame of reference for writing a case summary. I have directly referred to 18 of those articles in this essay.[6] In addition to these

---

[4]Like Lexis–Nexis, ProQuest's alternative press database is accessible by institutional subscription only at http://apw.softlineweb.com/

[5]These alternative press news items represented participants' perspectives, rather than the corporate or governmental perspectives represented in the mainstream press.

[6]Subsequently, in some cases, supplemental series searches using www.google.com and www.teoma.com were employed to confirm Web addresses for news articles.

published sources, I have referred to a transcript of an interview with an Iowa farmer who had planted StarLink corn. This interview is used to corroborate points made in other published reports here regarding the farmers as Aventis CropScience clients.[7]

Making sense of these news articles to interpret both how and why public relations practitioners acted in the Aventis CropScience case depends on textual analysis here. Gitlin (1980) explained that, "The basic strategies of textual analysis—selection, emphasis, and exclusion—enable the [scholar] to grapple with the 'complexity and contradictoriness of media artifacts'" (p. 303). The objective of this methodology is to produce a valid interpretation. Thus, theoretical validity, or "construct" validity, offers a method for evaluating the correctness of an interpretive analysis. The theoretical framework previously presented has served to define the coding categories used to select news stories for inclusion in the case study as well as to define the terms of analysis. The demonstration of a significant resonance between texts collected in this way as evidence and rigorously applied theory supports the validity of the following analysis.

THE STARLINK CASE

StarLink-brand seed corn was created by Aventis CropScience's American division based at Research Triangle Park by Aventis CropScience USA Holding, Inc. In 1999, it was licensed to the Garst Seed Co. of Slater, Iowa, for sale to farmers. Because it had been GM to include the protein, Cry9C, the seed attracted farmers with two key features: It was deadly to its main pest, the corn borer larva. It was engineered to be resistant to Aventis CropScience's Liberty Herbicide, which protects corn from insects and weeds (Robinson, 2002). In addition, StarLink represented a solution to pesticide- and herbicide-resistance developed by pests and weeds. As a result, corn-borer larvae that had become resistant even to other *Bt*, or *Bacillus thuringiensis*, corn would not be resistant to StarLink (Kaufman, 2000).[8]

As described later, the problem for Aventis CropScience lay in its approach to public relations in the distribution of this controversial biotechnology. In the face of challenges from regulatory agencies, environmental watchdog groups, farmers, and consumers, the apparent assumption by Aventis CropScience was that the corporation's "external" actions would have no significant internal effects.

---

[7]I thank the students of my Public Relations Campaigns section, Spring 2001, for their preliminary research on this topic, including this interview, which served as the incentive to begin this study.

[8]Bt is short for *Bacillus thuringiensis*, a naturally occurring organism that produces a protein fatal to the corn borer, an insect that can damage an entire crop if not dealt with.

Seeds of a Crisis: StarLink Goes to the Field

In the field, the immediate problem was that Cry9C was a suspected human allergen and a contaminant to corn varieties meant for human consumption
(Lucas, 2001). Environmental Protection Agency (EPA) doubts about the status
of Cry9C as an allergen kept the agency from approving the biotech variety for
human consumption up until—and beyond—the moment of its introduction to
American farmers. Indeed, at the time, it was the only GM crop that was restricted to use as animal feed (Kaufman, 2000).

The crisis came in the fall of 1999 when traces of StarLink corn in the food
stream led to the recall of some 300 food products such as taco shells, cornmeal,
and corn dogs (Brasher, 2001a; Cox, 2000; Hesman, 2000). Because Aventis
CropScience had sold the seed corn for cultivation as human food without first ob-
taining EPA approval, this amounted to the company's contamination of the global
food stream. By July 2001, the EPA had issued a ban on StarLink because it had
not been "proven safe for human consumption" (Brasher, 2001a, p. 4D).

More than just a series of public relations and marketing-led blunders, Aventis
CropScience's actions leading to the crisis suggest a flawed, if traditional, set of
assumptions about corporate public relations and what its practice can mean to the
corporation within the context of society. Although not expressed theoretically in
corporate terms, the Aventis CropScience position reflects assumptions associated
with "asymmetrical" practices of public relations. The first presumption of such
"monologic" communication style is that the institution's power can be maintained by standing apart (J. E. Grunig & L. A. Grunig, 1992).[9] As discussed previously in terms of the "duality of control," this approach is antithetical to the
concept of structuration (Giddens, 1984). Instead of presenting a holistic context
within which power and action are seen as commonly and recursively produced,
such unilateral action necessarily indicates a functionalist failure of corporate public relations actors to locate themselves within a common social context.

As late as December 2000, the EPA had hesitated to rule that genetically engineered corn was unfit for human consumption ("EPA Holds Off," 2001). From
there, the crisis quickly affected farmers, businesses, consumers, and environmentalists, who collectively charged federal regulatory agencies, including the United
States Department of Agriculture (USDA), Food and Drug Administration (FDA),
as irresponsible.

As a result of the contamination, farmers nationwide joined a class action lawsuit against Aventis CropScience charging that the company had been negligent in

---

[9]J. E. Grunig and L. A. Grunig (1992) offered concepts of "symmetrical" and "asymmetrical" public relations differentiate between dialogic and monologic patterns of communication. *Asymmetry*
means that the corporation acts to change its publics but not itself, while *symmetry* indicates two-way
change within a dialectical process.

failing to tell them that StarLink had been approved by the EPA only for animal feed because it contained the protein, Cry9C, a potential human allergen. Their suit, filed on December 1, 2000, in U.S. District Court in Chicago charged that StarLink-planting farmers allowed their crops to cross-pollinate with other, non-GM corn crops because of the company's negligence (Barboza, 2000). Farmers who planted StarLink lost their crops and their investments that year, when the FDA declined to approve the crop for human consumption.

In February 2001, two North Dakota farmers, Edward Olsen of Argusville and Gerald Greiger of Amenia, filed one of a number of class action suits around the nation, alleging that "Aventis CropScience knew that StarLink, being a cross-pollinating plant, would likely cross-pollinate with non-StarLink plants." They also alleged that

> Aventis CropScience knew that the 660-foot EPA-required buffer between StarLink crops and non-StarLink crops was inadequate … [and] … that Aventis CropScience knew it was not reasonable to expect that U.S. grain transportation and storage facilities would be capable of segregating StarLink corn and keeping it out of the food supply, according to a court document. (Grantier, 2001, p. 1B)

A spokesman for Garst Seed Co., of Slater, Iowa, the company that sold most of the StarLink seed in Iowa, reported that dealers had been advised of the restrictions, adding that a tag on seed bags told farmers to check a grower's guide about restrictions ("Iowa Growers," 2000). However, Iowa farmers generally disputed that account. One farmer, Douglas Radke, reported that his Garst sales representative had told him that the GM corn would be approved for humans by harvest time. As evidence, Radke produced a tag from a Garst bag of the StarLink corn seed that he had bought. It read, "You are licensed upon purchase of this product only to produce forage or grain for feed *or food* or grain processing" (D. Radke, personal communication, March 15, 2001). Butler County farmer Jim Norton reported finding the same tag on seed corn he used to plant 115 acres on his Iowa farm ("Iowa growers," 2000).

Radke explained that the term, "food," means for "human consumption," where "feed" indicates animals, only. "The farmer's rule of thumb is you always read the tags, no matter what anyone tells you," Radke said, "I didn't worry" (personal communication, March 15, 2001.)

A spokesman for Iowa Attorney General Tom Miller, Bob Brammer, said the state attorney general's office received about a dozen calls from StarLink growers. "Most tell us they were not told of the restriction," Brammer said. Jim Erickson, manager of the Fredericksburg Farmers Co-Op and the dealer who had sold the seed to Norton also reported that the seed lacked any warning labels ("Iowa Growers," 2000).

At the same time, though, a "grower confirmation letter" posted on the Aventis CropScience Web site read, "As a reminder, StarLink corn is approved for domestic animal feed or domestic industrial non-food uses ONLY. You understand and support these restrictions on uses of StarLink corn through your participation in the SES (StarLink Enhanced Stewardship) program" (Aventis, 2000a). Apart from this notice, Aventis CropScience's media relations policy depended on maintaining an official silence (Barboza, 2000). On the face of it, the company's communication management was out of synch with its distributor, Garst, and its clients, the farmers.

Many food-processing companies took measures to ensure that GM corn did not enter the human food channel through their products. General Mills, Kellogg, ConAgra, and Archer–Daniels–Midland were forced to shut down facilities for tests or turn away grain (Cox, 2000). Despite their efforts to ease the public's concern for their corn products, General Mills' stock prices declined and Taco Bell Corp.'s sales declined, due to negative publicity for having used GM contaminated shells (Spector & Martin, 2000).

Biotechnology As a Contested Idea

Prior to the StarLink food contamination event, the broader problem for the global biotechnology industry had been gaining public acceptance for its controversial products. In plain language, because genetic engineering means manipulating life forms to provide desirable products for human purposes, public responses have been complicated. In the world of food production, this means anything from insect-resistant Bt corn to the wine fermentation processes using biotechnology. Still, regulatory agencies and consumers often had contested the safety of GM food. In this case, the Bt corn was detected in Iowa crops by a Genetic Id, an environmental watchdog group (Kaufman, 2000).

In response to the public's anxieties, the corporate message from Aventis CropScience was blunt: The technology works. From their empirical perspective, the application of scientific logic to transfer beneficial genetic traits from one plant species to another in order to enhance or protect the plant represented a kind of essential truth, one with enormous capital potential. As presented, the Aventis CropScience position held that, although biotechnological techniques had become more sophisticated, the science of genetic modification was not new. Rather, farmers had been improving plants through the use of hybridization for centuries by selectively breeding two ideal plants to create a new plant with a higher yield less susceptible to disease (Mackey & Santerre, 2000).

Following this logic, the contemporary biotechnology of StarLink seems more dependable. Under laboratory conditions, researchers extract a desired gene from the cell of one plant by "cutting" along the DNA strand. The gene is then "pasted" into the DNA strand of the other plant cell. This creates a "plasmid" containing the new gene, which then can be used to produce new plants with the desired gene. In most cases, this gene helps protect against insect infestations or the use of chemicals such as herbicides and insecticides. Some plants are also engineered for higher yields (Biotechterms.org, n.d.).

According to the scientific logic of GM agriculture, Aventis CropScience was correct. In the case of StarLink brand corn, the validity of the science was not in question: The genetic modifications could do what they were supposed to do. Yet, treating science as objective fact and negotiating its acceptance amid broader cultural meaning are not the same thing. As the hue and cry from environmentalists, farmers, consumers, and regulatory agencies indicated, Aventis CropScience's public relations definition of this new science had not been accepted beyond its walls.

In November 2000, Aventis CropScience issued a press release under the heading, "StarLink—not a health or safety issue." Although acknowledging that StarLink had not been approved for human consumption by the EPA, the release also sought to defend Aventis CropScience's position regarding the meaning of biotechnology. It read, in part:

> On October 25, 2000 Aventis CropScience submitted a new evaluation of safety information on StarLink corn that recommends regulatory officials grant a time-limited approval for a presence of the corn in human food. The new submission demonstrates that consumer exposure to food products containing StarLink Cry9C protein—even under worst-case scenarios—is many thousands of times smaller than that required to sensitize and lead to a later allergic reaction. (Status Report on StarLink, 2000b, p. 1)

While retrenching to the pristine logic of positivism, the release also denied speculation in news reports that Aventis CropScience's losses related to StarLink would amount to as much as $1 billion reported in the press.

StarLink: Damage and Response

After reports were released showing StarLink in supermarket products (Kaufman, 2000), the company removed the corn variety from the market and took steps to find all remaining StarLink. As of February 2001, the company had located 99% of the 2000 StarLink harvest and had taken steps to ensure that all of the StarLink corn was fed to livestock or used to produce ethanol. Aventis CropScience spokesperson James Gray said the company had identified 916 farmers who had grown StarLink corn, another 598 farmers who had crops affected by cross-pollination, and 266 grain elevators that had handled StarLink corn (Cox, 2000; Glover, 2001).

As the scope of the crisis became apparent for Aventis CropScience, the potential penalties increased. At the end of December 2001, farmers who had not planted StarLink corn filed a class action suit in Cedar Rapids, Iowa, and Chicago against Aventis CropScience. The suit sought "nationwide class action status for the non-StarLink farmers, as well as compensatory and punitive damages from Aventis CropScience." It further alleged that there had been "widespread contamination of the U.S. corn crop by the StarLink product, both through cross-pollination of corn crops in farmers' fields as well as in grain elevators and other corn storage facilities" (Lucas, 2001). As congressional hearings were held, trade and consumer associations, such as the National Corn Growers Association, the Consumer's Union, and the Consumer Federation of America, found themselves on the same side against this contamination of the food stream (Anthan, 2000, 2001; Butler, 2000).

In response to the lawsuit, Aventis CropScience made plans to compensate the approximately 2,000 American farmers who planted StarLink corn and recoup the financial losses they would face as a result of StarLink's presence in the food supply (Cox, 2000). The buyback plan was drafted in cooperation with Iowa Attorney General Tom Miller and the attorneys general of 16 other states to purchase unmarketable StarLink corn from farmers' fields (Gibson, 2001). The company would buy back any GM corn from Iowa farmers for 25 cents per bushel. Corn mixed with the GM kernels was eligible for a 5 cent per bushel payment, if it had been purchased for livestock feed, 10 cents if the corn were sold to approved industrial outlets (Gibson, 2001).[10]

In 2000, StarLink had been planted by approximately 3,000 growers on approximately 350,000 acres. In all, Aventis CropScience ended up buying approximately 40 million bushels of contaminated corn (StarLink Growers, 2000). It was the prospect of implementing this buyback plan that produced estimates of costs between $100 million and $1 billion to Aventis CropScience (Sissell, 2001).

In 2001, market growth for biotech crops fell off significantly, while the effects of the StarLink contamination crisis lingered. However in 2002 the rate of biotech corn planting rose by 23% to 25.3 million acres, or 32% of the national corn crop, according to USDA estimates. GM cotton and soybeans also experienced increases in market share, although not as high (U.S. Farmers, 2002). In the end, Aventis CropScience's mishandling of StarLink did not seem to have derailed the trend in GM agri-industry, although it did cost the company its lucrative share in that growing market. By November 2001, the crisis had led Aventis CropScience's management to divest its CropScience division in a sale to the German pharmaceutical giant, Bayer ("Bayer Agrees," 2001).

---

[10]In some cases, Aventis CropScience agreed to buy corn grown within the required 660-ft buffer area next to neighboring farms, as well. In addition to farmers, operators of grain elevators where GM corn had become commingled with natural kernels were eligible for compensation from Aventis CropScience (Gibson, 2001).

In March 2002, Aventis CropScience and Garst were parties to a $9 million class-action lawsuit on behalf of consumers, along with Kraft Foods Co. of Glenview, Illinois; Azteca Foods Inc., of Chicago, Illinois; Azteca Milling, Co. of Edinburg, Texas; and a sister company, Mission Foods Co. (Robinson, 2002). The Iowa-grown corn found its way through Midwestern fields and Texas millers into grocery stores as Taco Bell and Safeway brand taco shells, Kellog's corn dogs, and Kash n' Karry White Corn Tortilla Chips, among some 300 grocery products made of corn (Hesman, 2001; Kaufman, 2000). Although no allergic reactions were confirmed, the force of the consuming public's fear had grown quickly (Hesman, 2001).

Ultimately, in spite of the buyback effort, Aventis sold its agricultural division, CropScience, to the German company, Bayer at a loss (Fick, 2001).[11] In that sense, the "crisis" became defined not only in terms of the damage to others working along the food growing and manufacturing industry, but as the end of Aventis's capital stake in a growing industry. This embodies Giddens's (1984) concept of the "duality of structure," where it is impossible for an institution to escape the effects of its own actions.

Although the presence of the StarLink corn in the U.S. food supply did not impact domestic corn prices or the export market, it did revive the national debate on biotechnology and GM food. After the corporation had taken steps to clean up the contamination and address injured parties, many consumers and activist groups continued to raise questions about the ethics of genetically modifying any organisms as well as the health risks and environmental consequences of biotechnology.

ANALYSIS

StarLink's definition as an "agricultural technology" seems unambiguous. However, the general reactions of various publics to bio-engineered food were more complicated than that, based as they were on alternative ideological interpretations of the scientific "facts." The StarLink case demonstrates this conflict as an ideological contest between the positivism of bioengineering, on the one hand, and the variously hostile interpretations of those affected by the contamination, on the other hand.

---

[11]Founded December 15, 1999, the division had been the result of a merger between the German company, Hoechst, and the French Rhone–Poulenc, two leading European concerns in agriculture and pharmaceuticals. Aventis's global headquarters are located in Strasbourg, France. By September 2000, its fate was sealed as StarLink corn approved only as animal feed was detected in products for human consumption (Kaufman, 2000).

According to Hesman (2000), Aventis was one of several biotech company to separate its agricultural and pharmaceutical businesses from pharmaceutical divisions in 2000. Pharmacia Corp. recently spun off Creve Coeur-based Monsanto Co. In addition, Novartis AG and AstraZeneca PLC dropped their farm chemical divisions to create Syngenta AG.

According to Berger (1999), public relations is an inherently ideological practice. He qualified it as based on "three aspects of ideology—distortion, legitimation, and terrain of struggle" (p. 191). Where he asserted that the first two serve a functional purpose of preserving corporate power by using "meaning in the service of power" (Thompson, 1990, p. 7), his third concept of a "terrain of struggle" suggested an instability for organizational meaning that is due to multiple, dialectical processes (Berger, 1999, pp. 191–194). Because traditional functionalist assumptions cannot guarantee corporate predominance—as shown in the current case—Berger's latter concept offers an important point of departure from any functionalist model of public relations, implicit or otherwise.

Where Berger (1999) defined public relations as "neither strictly functional nor intentionally symmetrical, … [but] ideological" (p. 191), Giddens's (1984) theory of structuration offers public relations practitioners a way to understand the interplay of ideological positions as an interpretable context, rather than as a set of possible outcomes to be projected from a static corporate position. In this sense, although dominance may be an outcome for strong institutions, it cannot be the premise for its own reproduction and should not be the goal.

Rather, negotiating public relations in this way would mean changing the ways in which practitioners envision communication within the corporate effort. It would mean accepting that a more effective communication strategy would involve recognizing that actions lead to unintended—and recursive—consequences. Although Aventis lost its business in this example, the broader suggestion here is one of unforeseeable opportunity for public relations to take unpredictable but potentially positive steps within strategies as unfolding, interpretive processes.

By extension, adopting the structuration approach means changing the temporality assumed by contemporary public relations practitioners. Instead of expecting their strategies and tactics to involve static actions and equally static reactions, as indicated by the causal assumptions and quasi-empiricism of traditional public relations management models (e.g., J. E. Grunig & Hunt, 1984), identifying public relations practice within a process of structuration would mean taking a more interpretive approach to the multiple, unintended outcomes of social interactions as points of entry into structuring dialogues. By recognizing public relations as taking part within and *as* such flux, it should be more possible to participate in the definition of new social "rules," for example, about the acceptability (or not) of bioengineered food (Giddens, 1984).

In effect, the paradigm shift prescribed here calls for the recognition at a "professional" level of this "intellectual" concept to approach public relations (Dozier & Lauzen, 2000). To make this change, the work and social routines implicitly created by practitioners' institutional interactions with consumers, activists, and even regulatory agencies will have to change radically. A benefit of becoming conscious of the holism of social reproduction by escaping such "imbedded" routines would be the realization agency and "action" (Giddens, 1984).

Such an awareness would also enable practitioners to address activists, activists who "pose a paradox for the nomothetic model of public relations theory" (Dozier & Lauzen, 2000, p. 3). In this case, several activist groups presented "unintended consequences" by taking aim at the issue of food contamination, including the Friends of the Earth, Gen id, and Ending Destructive Genetic Engineering (Hauben, 2000). Their action was sparked when another group, the Genetically Engineered Food Alert, identified StarLink corn in taco shells using scientific and public relations techniques that quickly overwhelmed Aventis CropScience's professionals (Hauben, 2000). If the Aventis CropScience professionals had been approaching their work from an interpretive perspective, it would have been more likely for them to have responded to the ensuing conflicts opportunistically as "structuring moments," where some change is certain although its outcome may be unclear (Giddens, 1984).

Given the call for such new competencies, the key for corporate public relations practitioners would be to interpret the social dialectic of conflict as a process of structuration. In that sense, it is essential to understand the difference between defending "principles" of social organization and changing "rules" about social practices (Giddens, 1984). In this example, both the activists and the Aventis CropScience Corporation were contesting a key principle: The corporate prerogative to pursue its markets, here by introducing GM crops. Although the "rule" at stake was whether to accept GM crops, the broader principle of who could operate at that level of capitalism was not.

As a case in point, the only extinction that Aventis faced—the demise of its CropScience division—came as a result of the company's failure to recognize and participate in the holistic context that demanded dialogue within an ideologically diverse context. In such a structuring dialogue, competent public relations practitioners should be aware of the balance inherent in the metacontext described by Giddens (1984) as the "dialectic of control," where the holistic atmosphere of the dialectic shapes the participants as much as they might try to shape the outcome. In that sense, dialogue would not be conflated with "parity," but understood as a more open and reflexive process of interpretation and action.

CONCLUSIONS

Giddens (1984) theory of structuration can contribute to a more meaningful practice of public relations by promoting the awareness that power—both as explicit social meaning for institutions and their constituents, and as the basis for the continued redefinition of the common social context—is produced and reproduced within such structuring contexts. Public relations can become a medium for that more fully realized action.

By interpreting the Aventis CropScience case as subject to a duality of control, however unrecognized by the principals, I hope to have shown that it would be possible for public relations practitioners to reinterpret their work within the dialectic of structuration. As a result, approaching public relations—whether in the university classroom or in the workplace—by understanding the dialogic context of structuration makes it more likely that professionals will lead corporate participation in society with a reflexive and empathic regard for their stake in the social process of rules making that is structuration (Giddens, 1984).

On those terms, making decisions about whether or how to engage new technologies like GM crops could be approached on entirely different bases. With hindsight, by setting aside the traditional prerogatives of functionalism—that is, to act principally on behalf of the corporate institution and its shareholders as global capitalists, constrained only by necessary attention to local legal or regulatory constraints—I imagine that Aventis CropScience might have found a slower and more complex, but ultimately more productive, approach to the circumstance they engaged by introducing StarLink to the market. It is possible that the market—producers, consumers, distributors, activists, and regulators—might have opened in otherwise unforeseeable ways. Based on the theory of structuration, public relations managers in future cases have the option to be more effective as interpretivists by seeking to understand and act on the continually changing nature of the institution's place in society.

REFERENCES

Althusser, L. (1971). *Lenin and philosophy and other essays.* New York: Monthly Review Press.
Anthan, G. (2000, November 5). StarLink could hasten shakeout—Seed firms to dwindle? *The Des Moines Register.* Retrieved March 25, 2001, from http://www.biotech-info.net/shakeout2.html
Anthan, G. (2001, January 12). Biotech policy "holds great peril." *The Des Moines Register.* Retrieved March 25, 2001, from http://www.biotech-info.net/iceberg.html
Aventis. (2000a, November 10). Aventis CropScience grower conformation letter. Retrieved March 25, 2001, from http://www.us.cropscience/aventis.comf/AventisCropScienceUS/Crop/Growerconfirmation_option2lett.ht
Aventis. (2000b, November 9). Aventis CropScience status report on StarLink. Retrieved March 25, 2001, from http://www.AventisCropScience.com/main/0,1003,EN-XX-30119-32810--FF.html
Baber, Z. (1991). Beyond the structure/agency dualism: An evaluation of Anthony Giddens' theory of structuration. *Sociological Inquiry, 61,* 219–230.
Barboza, D. (2000, December 3). Negligence suit is filed over altered corn. *The New York Times,* p. C2.
Bayer agrees to acquire Aventis CropScience CropScience. (2001, October 2). Aventis CropScience S.A. Press Release. Retrieved February 15, 2002, from http://www.Aventis CropScience.com/main/0,1003,EN-XX-10590-45177--,FF.html
Blau, P. (1977). *Inequality and heterogeneity.* New York: Free Press.
Berger, B. K. (1999). The Halcion affair: Public relations and the construction of ideological world view. *Journal of Public Relations Research, 11,* 185–203.
Berger, B. K. (2005). Power over, power with, and power to relations: Critical Reflections on public relations, the dominant coalition, and activism. *Journal of Public Relations Research, 17,* 5–27.
Biotechterms.org (n.d.) Retrieved March 20, 2003, from http://biotechterms.org/sourcebook/
Blakeslee, N. (2001, March 30). Banking on biotech: Is the latest food science from Aggie-land a lemon? *The Texas Observer, 93*(6), 6.

Brasher, P. (2001a, July 28). No StarLink corn will be allowed in food, EPA rules. *The Bismark Tribune*, p. 4D.

Brasher, P. (2001b, March 8). *Tests find unapproved corn in meat product.* Associated Press [Online]. Retrieved March 15, 2002, from Lexis–Nexis.

Butler, M. E. (2000, September 27). *Mandatory labeling of biotech foods debated at congressional hearing.* Dow-Jones Interactive: Publications Library [Online database]. Available from http://ptg.djnr.com//ccroot/asp/publib/story.asp

Cox, J. (2000, October 27). StarLink fiasco wreaks havoc in the heartland: Developer wants EPA to approve seed for food supply. *USA Today* [Online]. Retrieved March 23, 2001, from http://www.usatoday.com/usatonline /20011027/2787692s.htm

Dozier, D. M., & Lauzen, M. M. (2000). Liberating the intellectual domain from the practice: Public relations, activism, and the role of the scholar. *Journal of Public Relations Research, 12,* 3–22.

Durham, F. D. (2002). Anti-Communism, race, and structuration: Newspaper coverage of the labor and desegregation movements in the South, 1932–40 and 1953–61. *Journalism and Mass Communication Monographs 4,* 49–107.

EPA holds off on Starlink decision. (2001, December 24). The Associated Press [Online]. Retrieved March 15, 2002, from Lexis–Nexis.

Fick, J., (2001, September 4), Bayer near agreement to buy CropScience. *USA Today,* p. 1B.

Garfinkel, H. (1967). *Studies in ethnomethodology.* Englewood Cliffs, NJ: Prentice-Hall.

Gibson, R. (2001, January 24). Companies: Aventis CropScience unit in U.S. to reimburse StarLink losses—Farmers will get 25 cents per bushel of altered corn. Dow Jones Newswires [Online]. Retrieved February 15, 2002, from http://ptg.djnr.com/ccroot/ asp/publib/story_clean_cpy.asp?articles= WSJE01

Giddens, A. (1976). *The new rules of sociological method.* New York: Basic.

Giddens, A. (1979). *Central problems in social theory: Action, structure and contradiction in social analysis.* New York: Macmillan.

Giddens, A. (1984). *The constitution of society: Outline of the theory of structuration.* Berkeley: University of California Press.

Gitlin, T. (1980). *The whole world is watching.* Berkeley: University of California Press.

Glover, M. (2001, February 12). StarLink maker says all grain has been found. *The Jefferson City News Tribune Online Edition.* Retrieved March 15, 2002, from http://www.newstribune.com/stories/ 021301/bus_0213010028.asp

Goffman, E. (1959). *The presentation of self in everyday life.* New York: Doubleday.

Gramsci, A. (1971). *Selections from the prison notebooks* (Q. Hoare & G. N. Smith). New York: International.

Grantier, V. (2001, February 22). Farmers sue Aventis CropScience over impacts from modified corn; Plaintiffs allege Aventis CropScience knew that EPA required buffer was inadequate. *The Bismarck Tribune,* p. 1B.

Grunig, J. E., & Grunig, L. A. (1992). Models of public relations excellence. In J. E. Grunig (Ed.), *Excellence in public relations and communication management* (pp. 285–325). Hillsdale, NJ: Lawrence Erlbaum Associates, Inc.

Grunig, J. E., & Hunt, T. (1984). *Managing public relations.* New York: Holt, Rinehart, & Winston.

Hauben, L. (2000, Nov. 9). *The Santa Barbara Independent, (14)*728, p. 82.

Hesman, T. (2001, February 20). Biotech firms need to address emotional issues of consumers. *The St. Louis Post-Dispatch,* p. D2. Retrieved October 29, 2004, from http://www.plantuoguel-ph.ca/ safefood/archives/agnet-archives.htm

Holtzhausen, D. (2000). Postmodern values in public relations. *Journal of Public Relations Research, 12,* 93–114.

Holtzhausen, D., & Voto. R. (2002). Resistance from the margins: The postmodern public relations practitioner as organizational activist. *Journal of Public Relations Research 14,* 57–82.

Iowa growers: We weren't warned of biotech corn; StarLink: Aventis CropScience says that farmers should have known. (2000, October 26). *Telegraph Herald* (Dubuque, IA), p. C6.

Karlberg, M. (1996). Remembering the public in public relations research: From theoretical to operational symmetry. *Journal of Public Relations Research, 8,* 263–278.

Kaufman, M. (2000, September 18). Biotech critics cite unapproved corn in taco shells; Gene-modified variety allowed only for animal feed because of allergy concerns. *The Washington Post*, p. A02.

Kotler, P. (1982). *Marketing for non-profit organizations* (2nd ed.). Englewood Cliffs, NJ: Prentice-Hall.

Kotler, P., & Roberto, E. L. (1989). *Social marketing: Strategies for changing public behavior.* New York: Free Press.

Lucas, M. (2001, December 29). Cedar Rapids, Iowa, farmers' law suit looks to gain class-action status. *The Cedar Rapids Gazette.* Retrieved January 26, 2002, from Lexis–Nexus.

Mackey, M. A., & Santerre, C. R. (2000). Biotechnology and our food supply. *Nutrition Today.* Retrieved February 8, 2002, from http://www.findarticles.com/m0841/4_35/65013832/p1/article.jhtml

Mickey, T. J. (1997). A postmodern view of public relations: Sign and reality. *Public Relations Review, 23,* 271–284.

Miller, K. L. (2000). Common ground from the post-positivist perspective: From "straw-person" argument to collaborative coexistence. In S. R. Corman & M. S. Poole (Eds.), *Perspectives on organizational communication: Finding common ground* (pp. 47–67). New York: Guilford.

Motion, J., & Weaver, C. K. (2005). The discourse perspective for critical public relations research: Life sciences network and the battle for "truth." *Journal of Public Relations Research, 17,* 49–67.

Mouzelis, N. (1989). Restructuring structuration theory. *The Sociological Review, (37)*4, 613–635.

Parsons, T. (1949). *The structure of social action.* Glencoe, IL: Free Press.

Robinson, M. (2002, March 8). *Judge approves $9M settlement in engineered-corn suit.* Associated Press [Online]. Retrieved March 15, 2002, from Lexis–Nexis.

Roper, J. (2005). Symmetrical communication: Excellent public relations or a strategy for hegemony? *Journal of Public Relations Research, 17,* 69–86.

Schutz, P. (1972). *The phenomenology of the social world.* London: Heinemann.

Sewell, W. H., Jr., (1992). A theory of structure: Duality, agency, and transformation. *American Journal of Sociology, 98*(1), 1–29.

Sissell, K. (2001, January). Aventis CropScience to pay growers for grain mix-up. In *Chemical Week* [Online]. Retrieved March 15, 2002, from http://email.uiowa.edu/MBX/klgray/ID=3A9D642C/MSG:12

Spector, A., & Martin, R. (2000, December 18). Sales, hardships, biotech flap shellac Taco Bell operators. *Nation's Restaurant News.* Retrieved March 15, 2002, from Lexis–Nexis.

StarLink growers get premiums; questions still to answer. (2000, October 10). In *Progressive Farmer* [Online]. Retrieved March 9, 2003, from http://www.biotech-info.net/starlink_premiums.html

Status report on StarLink. (2000, November 9). *Aventis CropScience status report on StarLink.* Retrieved March 17, 2003, from http://www.aventis.com/main/page.asp?pageid=63336185872770551170&lang=en

Thompson, J. B. (1990). *Ideology and modern culture: Critical social theory in the era of mass communication.* Stanford, CA: Stanford University Press.

U.S. farmers will grow maore biotech crops. (2002, March 29). *Milwaukee Journal-Sentinel*, p. 9A.

Weaver, G. R., & Goia, D. A. (1994). Paradigms lost: Incommensurability versus structuralist inquiry. *Organizational Studies, 15,* 565–590.

Williams, R. (1977). *Marxism and literature.* Oxford, England: Oxford University Press.

Williams, R. (1980). *Problems in materialism and culture: Selected essays.* London: Verso and NLB.

JOURNAL OF PUBLIC RELATIONS RESEARCH, *17*(1), 49–67

A Discourse Perspective for Critical Public Relations Research: Life Sciences Network and the Battle for Truth

Judy Motion and C. Kay Weaver

Department of Management Communication
University of Waikato

Critical public relations scholarship is increasingly required to justify the contribution that is made to theory and practice. Within this article, an integrated political economy and discourse analysis is deployed to examine a progenetic engineering advocacy campaign conducted by the Life Sciences Network in New Zealand. The analysis demonstrates the value of examining the sociopolitical contexts in which public relations operates and the discourses that it seeks to produce or influence and thus provides a constructive foundation for further critical research.

James E. Grunig (2001) stated that "in a professional field such as public relations, I believe scholars must go beyond criticizing theories; they also have the obligation to replace theories with something better—an obligation that many critical scholars do not fulfil" (p. 17). Although many critical scholars claim that their work does indeed attempt to offer new ways of thinking about public relations—variously from postmodernist (Holtzhausen, 2000; McKie, 2001), cultural studies (Mickey, 1998), sociological (L'Etang & Pieckza, 1996), political economy (Miller & Dinan, 2000; Weaver & Motion, 2002), and critical discourse (Motion & Leitch, 1996; Weaver, 2001) perspectives—J. E. Grunig's comments are indicative of a need for critical researchers and theorists to more clearly outline how their approaches contribute to advancing not only public relations theory, but also research and practice.

In this article we demonstrate how critical public relations research can contribute to theorizing public relations practice by developing an understanding of how

Requests for reprints should be sent to Judy Motion, Department of Management Communication, University of Waikato, Private Bag 3105, Hamilton, New Zealand. Email: motionjm@waikato.ac.nz discourse is used to establish particular "regimes of truth" (Foucault, 1972/1980, p. 131). We build on the work of Motion and Leitch (1996) who argued that, "Public relations practitioners are ... discourse technologists who play a central role in the maintenance and transformation of discourse" (p. 298). In advancing this understanding of public relations practice, we argue that critical discourse analysis provides public relations scholars and practitioners with an ability to conceptualize public relations within the context of culture as a symbolic system where that system "itself is a crucial site in which power may be exercised, contested, negotiated, or resisted" (Switzer, McNamara & Ryan, 1999, p. 26). From this perspective, public relations is theorized as a legitimate tactic in the struggle for and negotiation of *power*. The task for the critical public relations scholar is to investigate how public relations practice uses particular discursive strategies to advance the hegemonic power of particular groups and to examine how these groups attempt to gain public consent to pursue their organizational mission.

We also argue that discourses deployed for public relations purposes can only be fully understood in relation to the political, economic, and social contexts in which they operate. Moreover, considering the wider cultural context of public relations practice enables researchers to fully theorize how publics are encouraged to conceptualize "the public interest" and support the public relations message in what J. E. Grunig (2001), following Dozier, L. A. Grunig, and J. E. Grunig (1995), described in the new contingency two-way model of public relations as a "win–win" situation for both client and publics.

Despite a number of critical scholars having argued that discourse theory provides valuable insights into public relations practice (Motion & Leitch, 1996, 2001; Weaver, 2001), none have actually demonstrated *how* that practice can be deconstructed through critical discourse research. In demonstrating precisely this, our article presents a discourse analysis of the Life Sciences Network campaign that has sought to promote an acceptance of genetic modification in New Zealand during the 2002 New Zealand national government elections.

Genetic modification (GM) is currently one of the most contentious of scientific applications and is a matter of major international debate and concern. Indeed, the very term *genetic modification* has been a matter of contestation and tends to be used by proponents of the science, whereas the term *genetic engineering* (GE) tends to be the preferred term of those opposed to the science. Many organizations and groups have argued that GM represents a significant advancement of scientific knowledge that can, for example, enhance agricultural output, reduce the need for pesticide use, and increase the shelf-life of foods and extract toxins and allergens from foods (Conner, 2000; Kettle, 2000). It is also claimed that GM research may offer medical breakthroughs in the treatment of, for instance, kidney disorders and diabetes (Kettle, 2000). Those who oppose GM technologies, and especially field trials and their commercial application, argue that there are vast unknown risks involved in this new science and that it could cause significant damage to not only the environment and bio-diversity but to the health and future of all species (see, e.g., Allen, 2000; Ho, 1999). Not surprisingly given the controversies that surround GM, the role that public relations has played in contributing to public knowledge about this science has also been highly criticized (Bruno, 1998; Weaver & Motion, 2002; see also Durham, 2005/this issue). Before examining that role in the context of the Life Sciences Network campaign, we outline the critical, discourse and political economy theories we draw on in our analyses of public relations practice.

CRITICAL THEORY PERSPECTIVES

Being critical, as Downing, Mohammadi, and Sreberny-Mohammadi (1995) stated,

> involves posing questions, including awkward and unpopular ones. It means not merely taking information for granted, at face value, but asking how and why these things come to be, why they have the shape and organisation they do, how they work and for whose benefit. (p. xx)

In public relations scholarship the dominant functional managerial perspective is reluctant to ask (and necessarily avoids) these types of questions that are all essentially about power. This is because, as Berger (2001/in this issue), Durham (2001/in this issue), and Roper (2001/in this issue) all separately and from different theoretical perspectives demonstrate, even though functional theorists assert that public relations has to take into account notions of public interest, ultimately such perspectives privilege the interests of organizations, the elite or dominant coalition and capital.

In contrast, critical approaches to the study of public relations are centrally concerned with issues of power. As Trujillo and Toth (1987) stated, such perspectives "treat organizations as ideological and material arenas for power, influence, and control; and they treat organizational publics as coalitions and constituencies, which have diverse needs, values, and perspectives" (p. 209). The value of critical perspectives is that they investigate how political, sociocultural, and economic conditions shape public relations practice (Holtzhausen, 2000) and determine the "sources of power and influence" (Mickey, 1998, p. 336) that public relations practitioners represent. Equally important are issues concerning how public relations practice itself might promote certain values that fit within particular political, economic, and cultural frameworks and modes of living, but not with others. This in turn leads to a questioning of the role of public relations within, and its responsibilities to, democratic society.

Key to understanding how public relations represents and promotes selected positions of truth and power is the examination of the discourse strategies deployed by practitioners. In public relations, discourse is deployed as a political resource to influence public opinion and achieve political, economic, and sociocultural transformation. Most simply, a discourse may be thought of as a set of statements. That set of statements or discourse, according to Foucault (1996), comprised "the existence of rules of formation for all its objects, for all its operations, for all its concepts, and for all its theoretical options"(p. 35). Thus, discourse is both symbolic and constitutive, structuring how we know, understand, speak about, and conduct ourselves in that world. As Fairclough (1992) explained, discourse is "a practice, not just of representing the world, but of signifying the world in meaning" (p. 64). Although we are in agreement with Philo and Miller (2001) that *not all* experiences are explained through and by discourses, we argue that the core business of public relations is to provide and shape the meanings for social, cultural political, and economic experiences to benefit the client organization.

Public relations practitioners "strategically deploy texts that facilitate certain socio-cultural practices and not others" (Motion & Leitch, 1996, p. 299). In doing so they are attempting to gain a position of power for the client by establishing a "regime of truth" (Foucault, 1972/1980, p. 131). The ultimate strategic aim of being the "voice of truth" is to gain public consent for particular material practices. Thus, the establishment of a regime of truth, is "linked in a circular relation with systems of power which produce and sustain it, and to effects of power which it induces and which extend it" (Foucault, 1972/1980, p. 131). Truth and power, therefore, are inextricably linked and serve to reinforce one another.

Foucault (1972/1980) conceptualized power as both organized and hierarchical within the context of clusters of relationships. The notion of power as relational was clarified by adding the element of strategy. That is, Foucault (1972/1980) saw individuals and organizations as deploying various discourse strategies to conform with, circumvent, or contest existing power relations. However, it is important to note that although the term *power* most usually carries pejorative connotations of domination, Foucault (1969/1972) conceived of power as positive and productive. Foucault (1969/1972) stated, "What makes power hold good, what makes it accepted, is simply the fact that it doesn't only weigh on us as a force that says no, but that it transverses and produces things, it induces pleasure, forms knowledge, produces discourse" (p. 119). From this perspective then, discourse is the vehicle through which power and truth circulate and the means by which public relations practitioners attempt to strategically maintain and reproduce the status quo or transform society. By employing a critical discourse lens in public relations research we are able to examine the role that public relations plays in attempting to promote organizational and social discursive shifts and transformations.

However, critical discourse analysis can have its weaknesses due to its predominantly textual focus. As Philo and Miller (2001) asserted "without an analysis of changes in social process and material conditions, a textualist has trouble in explaining why a discourse might have to be altered" (p. 44). Consequently discourses, and discourse transformations, have to be theorized in the context of their political and economic circumstances and changes to those circumstances. Indeed, for the critical public relations scholar "the meaning of the words and pictures are … discerned in relation to the economic and political environment in which they are represented" (Mickey 1998, p. 342). That is, the political landscape, relevant economic agendas, government legislation, and public policy initiatives all form part of the political economy context of public relations discourse practice.

Political economy theory "insists on the power of capital and the process of commodification as a starting point of social analysis" (Mosco, 1996, p. 25). It is an approach that requires posing questions that "focus attention on how the re-sources for cultural practice, both material and symbolic, are made available in structurally determined ways through the institutions and circuits of commodified cultural production, distribution and consumption" (Garnham, 1997, p. 72). Thus, a critical political economy perspective can highlight how public relations partici-pates in the attempt to manage or control these resources as a hegemonic strategy. By hegemony we mean the nonviolent struggle to maintain "economic, political, cultural and ideological" power (Fairclough, 1992, p. 92; see also Roper, 2005/this issue). To establish, maintain, or transform hegemonic power, public relations dis-course strategies are deployed to circulate ideas, establish advantageous relation-ships, and privilege certain truths and interests.

A key strategy in how public relations contributes to hegemonic power is the "ar-ticulation, disarticulation and rearticulation of elements in a discourse" (Fairclough, 1992, p. 93). Articulation, as Hall (1996) explained, is the connection or linking of two different elements "which can be rearticulated in different ways because they have no necessary 'belongingness'" (p. 53). Moffitt (1994) and, subsequently, Mo-tion and Leitch (1996), already identified the importance of articulation to public re-lations theory and practice. For public relations practitioners the value of articulating otherwise unconnected discourse elements together is that through this strategy they can articulate an image or idea with pre-existing attitudes or experi-ences that then will predispose an individual to accept that idea or image (Motion & Leitch, 1996, p. 300). It is through the analysis of articulation strategies that we can identify how public relations texts function within the political economy context.

A CRITICAL METHOD

Having outlined the theoretical perspectives that we bring to our critical analysis of public relations, we can now demonstrate how we apply those perspectives to the investigation of public relations practice.

In the analysis of the Life Sciences Network campaign a three-phase research approach was adopted. First, three research questions were identified: (a) What were the particular political and economic conditions that supported the produc-tion of the New Zealand Life Sciences Network campaign and whose interests were represented by the campaign? (b) What discourse strategies were deployed in the campaign? and (c) How did the campaign attempt to influence public opinion and/or policy agendas and material practice?

The second phase of the research investigated the political and economic structures and conditions of power and ownership that were the historical backdrop to the campaign. The scope of this part of the analysis was kept manageable by examining who or what organizations had a political or economic vested interest in GM in New Zealand—and especially in relation to the Life Sciences Network; where, when, and how GM featured in political and economic debates and events; and what material practices were sought by those with interests in the GM issue.

The third stage of the research comprised the close analysis of the Life Sciences Network campaign texts. Here, in keeping with the concerns of a critical political economy of communications, the aim was to identify how the

> discourses are [strategically] handled in the text, whether they are arranged in a clearly marked hierarchy of credibility which urges the audience to prefer one over others, or whether they are treated in a more even-handed and indeterminate way which leaves the audience with a more open choice. (Golding & Murdock, 1991, p. 27)

This discursive investigation entails asking *who* is used to express a particular viewpoint and *why* they are used to perform this discursive role, *which institutions*, if any, do they represent, and *what* are the positions and viewpoints from which they speak? After analyzing the campaign from this microdiscursive perspective, the researcher is in a position to conclude how the campaign discourse seeks to influence public opinion and ultimately hegemonic power and "truth."

Having outlined how we approached our analysis of the Life Sciences Network campaign, we now turn our attention to the substance of that analysis. First however, it is pertinent to provide some background detail on the Life Science Network and its campaign texts in order to provide an understanding of the aims of both the organization and the campaign.

THE LIFE SCIENCES NETWORK AND ITS CAMPAIGN TEXTS

The New Zealand Life Sciences Network formed in early 2000 just prior to the hearings of the New Zealand Royal Commission of Inquiry Into Genetic Modification to counter what it claimed to be "uninformed and unbalanced public debate where science was being misinterpreted and ignored by anti-genetic engineering groups and the media" (Hagar, 2002, p. 12). Its membership comprises Crown Research Institutes (AgResearch, Crop and Food Research, HortResearch, Forest Research), universities, commercial corporations, and industry lobby groups. All of these members have a financial interest in the research and application of GM. By joining together under the Life Sciences Network umbrella they were able to pool financial resources and coordinate a united pro-GM lobby voice. This aim is explicitly outlined in the Life Sciences Network (2002b) constitution that states that one of the organizational objectives is to provide:

> An active voice for the creation of a positive environment for responsible use of genetic modification with appropriate caution; accurate and timely information and advocacy to respond to issues related to biotechnology as they arise; assisting and obtaining the cooperation of organisations that will or may benefit from the application of genetic modification procedures. (para. 3.1.f)

The overall strategy of the Life Sciences Network (2002a) is to "undertake three strands of activity; public education, media education and political education about GE and GMOs [genetically modified organisms] and the role of biotechnology" (para. 5). It has done this by making representation to the Royal Commission and providing the media with access to "experts" able to talk on the GM issue, and through an Internet site that, as well as providing information about the Life Sciences Network, provides a press clippings service on news coverage of GM and information kits on GM.

It was during the New Zealand 2002 national government elections that the Life Sciences Network developed the public campaign that is the focus of our critical analysis. The campaign comprised a television commercial, two newspaper advertorials, and an Internet based GM information kit. In addition, paid for pro-GM kits and a toll free hotline both were made exclusively available to election candidates with the exception of the "anti-GM" Green and Alliance parties. Of these materials our analysis focuses on those specifically targeting the New Zealand general public: the two newspaper advertorials and the Internet GM information kit. Although the television commercial also formed part of the public education strategy of the campaign, we have not included it in the analysis as it was only 5-sec long and simply encouraged viewers to read the newspaper advertorials.

The two newspaper advertorials that we analyze were published during the period of the election campaign—one at its outset and the other 3 days prior to polling. Both featured statements from expert opinion leaders to make a case for GM. The first advertorial (Life Sciences Network, 2002e) appeared in the *Waikato Times,* one of New Zealand's highest circulation regional papers. It was entirely text based and featured a quotation from the founder of Greenpeace, Patrick Moore, which took up one side of a double page, while information about the safety of GM was presented on the other side.

The second advertorial (Life Sciences Network, 2002d)—a single page spread—appeared in 21 national and regional newspapers and focused on GE research. Although this advertorial also was text intensive, the top right quarter featured a medium close-up photograph of a young woman in a white laboratory coat with the caption "Dr Margy Gilpin, Plant Biotechnologist and victim of sabotage." A second long-shot image of a smiling Gilpin in a dark jacket and skirt also featured at the bottom of the advertorial just left of center adjacent to the highlighted statement "Approved use of GE is safe." This advertorial reveals the story of Gilpin's laboratory based GE research that was "destroyed by saboteurs: anti GE fanatics." As we discuss next in our analysis of the text, the advertorial contains further statements from Gilpin about the safety of GE products and unattributed assertions that GE technology is of critical importance to New Zealand's future economic prosperity.

The third text included in our critical analysis of the Life Sciences Network public relations campaign is the Internet based information kit on genetic engineering (Life Sciences Network, 2002c). It is in this kit entitled "GM—The public's right to choose" that the most extensive explanation of GM and what are presented as the issues surrounding the science are given. One of the key aims of the entirely text-based kit is to provide communities that are considering going GM-free with information on the implications of doing so. The kit highlights the difficulties for local body authorities considering enforcing a GM-free zone.

Clearly, the Life Sciences Network undertakes many other public relations efforts such as lobbying. However, the publication of the advertorials during the election offered an opportunity to specifically reflect on the public education aspect of the campaign.

POLITICAL ECONOMY CONTEXT OF THE LIFE SCIENCES NETWORK CAMPAIGN

The Life Sciences Network campaign and the range of discourses used in that campaign can be fully understood only in relation to a wider set of political and economic practices that have shaped New Zealand's sociocultural and political landscape since the mid 1980s. Since 1984, New Zealand has pursued a right wing, neo-liberal economic agenda of privatization of central and local government services, market liberalization, and deregulation. This also has involved the promotion of foreign investment in New Zealand and, through the General Agreement on Tarriffs and Trade and the World Trade Organization, commitments have been made to free trade (Jesson, 1999; Kelsey, 1997, 2002; Weaver & Motion, 2002). This neo-liberal economic agenda was begun under a Labour Party government and then furthered under three consecutive National government terms. Under one of these National Party governments the Crown Research Institutes (CRIs), which, as we have stated, are members of the Life Sciences Network, were created "to carry out and promote research of excellence which would benefit New Zealand" (Kelsey, 1997, p, 121). More recently the CRIs have developed significant involvement and interest in GM research.

At the 1999 general election the Labour Party did not gain sufficient seats to secure a majority government and so formed a coalition government with the Alliance Party and depended on the seven Green Party Members of Parliament to support it on issues of confidence and supply (Kelsey, 2002). This gave the Green Party considerable leverage to pursue their environmental policies that, broadly, seek to maintain "New Zealand's clean, green image" (Fitzsimons, 2000, p. 196). In particular they have placed a priority on ensuring that New Zealand remain GM-free by not permitting commercial application of GM and GMOs. They also successfully campaigned for the establishment of the Royal Commission of Inquiry into GM in New Zealand. During the Royal Commission a moratorium on the release of GMOs was put in place until August 31, 2001.

Reporting on its findings in July 2001, the Royal Commission rejected the idea that New Zealand should remain GM-free. It concluded that "it would be unwise to turn our back on the potential advantages on offer, but we should proceed carefully, minimising and managing risks" (Royal Commission on Genetic Modification, 2001). The Royal Commission recommended that New Zealand keep its options open in relation to GM and loosen barriers to low-risk GM applications while calling for an increased regulatory framework for high-risk applications. With the reporting of the Royal Commission came an extension of the moratorium until October 2003 to enable the establishment of appropriate regulatory monitoring bodies for GM and GMO applications.

In August 2001 GM and biotechnology science research was discursively repositioned from that of an environmental issue to an economic one following a major 3-day "Catching the Knowledge Wave" Conference staged in Auckland and cochaired by the Prime Minister and the Vice Chancellor of the University of Auckland. The conference marked a significant attempt to promote public, political, and business discussion about transforming New Zealand into a knowledge society (Kelsey, 2002). As part of the Knowledge Wave initiative that followed the conference the government developed a Growth and Innovation Framework comprising three task forces: the biotechnology taskforce, the creative industries taskforce, and the information communication technologies taskforce. Each of these taskforces represented industries that the government considered of primary importance to New Zealand's economic growth. Of specific relevance here is the biotechnology task force that investigates ways of enhancing scientific research, development, and production in the biotechnology sector. It is in relation to this political and economic agenda that the Life Sciences Network campaign was able to promote biotechnology as central to New Zealand's economic prospects. Indeed, the campaign itself actually encourages audiences to understand a pro-GM stance as vital to the future development and well being of the country's economy in stating:

If we do not allow safe research to continue in New Zealand, we all pay the price. To cease the hard work would have an unprecedented negative impact on our economy and on our critical position in the knowledge economy. (Life Sciences Network, 2002d, p. 8)

In using the term *knowledge economy* the Life Sciences Network articulated a pro-GM position with the Government's agenda to develop New Zealand as a knowledge economy.

In May 2002 GM once again became a prominent environmental and political issue following the Green Party's refusal to support the Labour Government's passing of the Hazardous Substances and New Organisms (Amendment) Bill (Ministry for the Environment, 2004), which established an automatic expiry of the October 2003 moratorium on GM. This created considerable tensions between the Government and the Green Party that led to the coalition government becoming unstable. Consequently, on June 11, Prime Minister Helen Clark called a snap election for July 27 anticipating that, given that the Labour Party was proving very popular in the polls, Labour would be returned into office with a majority Government.

During the election campaign, GM was a key policy issue for debate and one that political commentators believed could significantly influence voting. It was in this context that the Life Sciences Network put out their media advertorial campaign. On June 22 it placed the Patrick Moore advertorial in the *Waikato Times* (Life Sciences Network, 2002e) and on July 24 placed the Margy Gilpin advertorial in both the national and regional press (Life Sciences Network, 2002d). However, the advertorials became a focus of some political and media controversy when *The New Zealand Herald* featured reports detailing that they had been paid for through a $180,000 fund set up by Life Sciences Network members, which included the Government funded CRIs, AgResearch and Crop and Food Research, (Collins, 2002a), and the University of Auckland's commercial arm "Uniservices" (Collins, 2002b). It was suggested that what could be regarded as a Government supported pro-GM campaign was intended to dissuade voters from giving their support to the Green Party in the election (Collins, 2002b).

In terms of its contribution to public understanding and knowledge of the GM issue during the election campaign, it can be argued that, from a public relations perspective, the Life Sciences Network campaign performed a perfectly legitimate role in informing the public of alternative views on GM that contrasted to the anti-GM position advocated by the Green Party. On the other hand the Life Sciences Network message can be viewed as a political campaign supporting government policy agendas, and one that is funded by the taxpayer. Furthermore, the timing of the campaign's second advertorial, appearing as it did 3 days before the national election, could be interpreted as an attempt to boost votes for pro-GM political parties and an attempt to intervene in the democratic process. This was certainly a criticism directed at the campaign by the coleader of the Green Party, Jeanette Fitzsimons, who argued, "I don't think it is appropriate for government research institutes to get into funding political campaigns" (as cited in Collins, 2002a). From the Government perspective, Peter Hodgson, the Minister of Science (in a radio interview), argued that the Life Science Network campaign had "nothing to do with politics" (as cited in Clark, 2002). However, as our discourse analysis now will demonstrate, the content of the Life Sciences Network campaign was inherently political.

DECONSTRUCTING THE ADVERTORIAL DISCOURSE

As we have indicated, a constitutional objective of the Life Sciences Network was to "influence the development of a positive public policy environment" (Life Sciences Network, 2002b, para. 3.1.d). Creating this positive public policy environment required a public opinion base that supported GM research for medicine and agriculture. To achieve this opinion base, the campaign adopted particular discourse strategies designed to counter what it termed "misinformation surrounding the debate" (Life Sciences Network, 2002e, p. 22). "Experts" were used to express an "informed" position supporting GM. The first advertorial quoted Patrick Moore as stating, "I believe the campaign of fear against genetically modified foods is based mostly on fantasy" (Life Sciences Network, 2002e, p. 22). Thus, a highly credible opinion leader on environmental issues is presented as supporting the need for a factually based debate on GM.

The advertisement then provides "facts" about public perceptions of safety. It states that

Last year 5594 New Zealand kids were injured at school. 30 New Zealanders died after driving into power poles. And 83 New Zealanders came home with Dengue Fever. By comparison, in some 20 years, not one health issue involving GM products has ever been substantiated. Not one. (Life Sciences Network, 2002e, p. 22)

These figures encourage the reader to consider socially accepted mundane everyday activities as involving elements of health risk that cannot be controlled and have a low probability of occurrence. In contrast GM is presented as having no known health risks. In effect the advertorial attempts to make a nonsense of objections to GM given that New Zealanders continue to participate in activities that do carry risk, but will not entertain the idea of GM technology that according to the text has only positively "contributed to many significant advances in medicine including much-improved human insulin for diabetics" (Life Sciences Network, 2002e, p. 22). In using this risk discourse the Life Sciences Network attempted to expose "a gulf between knowledge and decision, between the chain

of rational arguments and the course of action which attempts to resolve the di-
lemma" (Beck, 2000, p. xii). The advertorial seeks to close the knowledge gap
that people have regarding the health and safety risks of GM.

The advertorial also contains a highlighted text box that shifts the rational argument on GM to an emotive level in stating that "the only thing about the approved
use of GM technology that will make you sick is the misinformation surrounding
the debate" (Life Sciences Network, 2002e, p. 22). Thus the dangers of GM are
discursively constructed as having no basis in reality and anti-GM arguments are
positioned as "the real danger" to health. The advertorial then concludes in large
bold type "Approved use of GM is safe." In these terms the advertorial attempts to
establish a regime of truth about the safety of GM with the Life Sciences Network
as the arbiter of that truth.

The second advertorial repeats this safety message about GM. However, in this
second text the campaign used the term *GE* instead of *GM*. It could be argued that
this was done because this second advertorial focused largely on the GE debate
and anti-GE activism. In the text, GE is primarily (although not always) articulated
with distortions of truth. Indeed this point is emphasized through the advertorial's
headline banner that states "In the GE debate, the facts have been modified beyond
recognition" (Life Sciences Network, 2002d, p. 8). Although intended as a humor-
ous play on words to entice the reader to engage with the full text of the advertorial,
this headline discursively constructs the anti-GE position as hindering open and
honest debate. The anti-GE position is also presented as a highly emotional and
politicized discourse that creates unwarranted fear of GE technology.

In this text, Margy Gilpin brings scientific credibility to the advertorial message
that "there is no sane basis for the horror stories being promoted by certain,
anti-GE factions" (Life Sciences Network, 2002d, p. 8). The advertorial explains
that Gilpin was involved in GE research on potatoes for the CRI, Crop and Food
Research, and she is constructed as an intellectual whose research had "earned her
the right to present her results at the prestigious International Association of Plant
Tissue Culture Biotechnology. A career dream" (Life Sciences Network, 2002d, p.
8). However, although Gilpin is clearly set up as a scientific expert on GE, she is
also presented as a "mother of two young children" and a victim whose "entire [GE
research] crop was targeted and destroyed" (Life Sciences Network, 2002d, p. 8).
Thus, the reader is invited to trust Gilpin's message about GE from several *credible* positions. First she is an internationally recognized scientist whose work could
make an important contribution to the economic future of New Zealand. Second
she is positioned as a mother of children who, the reader is encouraged to assume,
would not put her children's health at risk by promoting GE if it were not safe. In
positioning Gilpin as a mother the text also encourages the reader to see her as an
"ordinary citizen" thereby reducing the gap between scientists and citizens en-
abling the reader to identify and empathize with her. Thirdly she is positioned as a
rational and knowledgeable person who was investigating "facts" about GE and

its potential health and agricultural applications, but whose work was destroyed by *emotional and irrational fanatics.*

Foucault (1972/1980) explained that the political economy of truth is centered on scientific discourse and that "it is necessary to think of the political problems of intellectuals not in terms of 'science' and 'ideology,' but in terms of 'truth' and 'power'" (p. 132). From this perspective, Gilpin's role is that of conveyer of truth and the advertorial can itself be considered as part of a "battle about the status of truth and the economic and political role its plays" (Foucault, 1972/1980, p. 132). That is, the text seeks to normalize GM and establish the Life Sciences Network perspective as the requisite truth about GM that has to achieve hegemonic ascendancy if New Zealand is to take political and economic advantage of this scientific technology.

In performing a discursive role within the advertorial, Gilpin presents the pro-GE position as one that emerges out of a rational considered analysis of factual scientific research findings, although no scientific facts about GE are presented. In contrast, anti-GE campaigners are depicted as little more than Luddite criminals whose destruction of Gilpin's crop not only destroyed her career chances, but possibly also New Zealand's future position in the global knowledge economy. The advertorial stated:

> New Zealand is in a very good position to be the world leader in GE technology. Scientists have been studying the safety and potential of crops since the first field trials at Lincoln in 1988 but we risk losing our place in the knowledge wave by not allowing continued research. People need to be able to make choices about the food they eat, by being informed with accurate information. (Life Sciences Network, 2002d, p. 8)

This statement clearly positions anti-GE campaigners as putting New Zealand's future prosperity at risk as well as attacking cherished liberal ideologies of an individual's right to choose and freedom from censorship—in this case the censorship of research activity. It also serves, as we have argued previously, to articulate the pro-GE discourse of the Life Sciences Network with that of current government policy. Yet underlying the statement are also appeals to notions of truth and objectivity. By inviting New Zealanders to return to a "rational" and "objective" consideration of GE technologies, rather than what is presented as the emotional and political anti-GE position, the Life Sciences Network reduced the complexity of debate around GE to the simple point that "in the last 20 years, no health issue involving consumption of GE products has ever been substantiated, even though an incredible amount of effort has gone into looking for potential problems" (Life Sciences Network, 2002d, p. 8). Thus, the advertorial repeated the safety assurance in the first advertorial and invited readers to consider that, in fact, the potential health and economic benefits of GE technologies outweigh any risks that they might pose.

Like the Life Sciences Network advertorials, the organization's Web pages also promoted GM technologies through very specific discursive lenses. The information kit lays out the issues around GM according to the Life Sciences Network's own agenda. These issues are detailed on the first page of the kit as (a) the relationship between organic farming and GM, (b) liability and safeguards, (c) health issues, (d) GM in the food chain, and (e) environment and sustainability.

In outlining the relationship between organic farming and GM the information kit explains that currently farmers have a freedom to choose which type of crop to farm according to what best suits their land and their individual expertise. This is contrasted with a possible future scenario where in a GM-free zone, "the ideological perceptions of other members of the community or the local body authority" (Life Sciences Network, 2002c, p. 3) determine the nature of their farming. The kit thus implies that in a GM-free zone, individual freedom of choice will be eliminated and farmers will find themselves powerless because they are "locked into a particular type of crop" (Life Sciences Network, 2002c, p. 3). Similarly, it is said:

> Residents in a GM-free zone would no longer have access to medicines that were genetically modified or produced by genetically modified organisms. At present this includes the cholera vaccine and the insulin used by diabetics in New Zealand. Would these residents be forced to move house to another local body or would the authorities turn a blind eye to doctors who smuggled supplies in to the zone and administered them to residents after hours? (Life Sciences Network, 2002c, p. 9)

We would argue that these assertions comprise a campaign of fear that is being waged against GM-free communities and that they are using the very same emotive and scare mongering tactics that their advertorials critique. This is evident in the images evoked by the information kit's suggestion that the establishment of GM-free communities would require the isolation and surveillance of physical communities. It is stated:

> Border posts would need to be set up to stop residents and visitors deliberately or inadvertently entering with GM organisms. For example, neighbouring farmers may enter the area with seeds on their boots or clothing and residents may be tempted to smuggle GM medicines in. Border checks would be a huge hassle for residents and visitors and a big expense for the local body authorities. (Life Sciences Network, 2002c, p. 9)

In this statement the Life Sciences Network encouraged the New Zealand public to perceive a GM-free position as threatening the New Zealand way of life—creating divisions among communities and instituting a regime of surveillance. In constructing such a scenario the campaign predicts a disutopian future that is clearly designed to counter the discursive construction of the organic and authentically clean green and safe New Zealand environment used by anti-GM lobby groups. In effect, we would argue that the kit is designed to ensure that local body authorities do not undermine national pro-GM policy and legislation by succumbing to anti-GM discourses.

The GM-free scenario is also constructed as problematic under the liability considerations explored in the information kit. It is argued that current New Zealand common law can adequately deal with the introduction of GMOs into the country, but that the real liability issues lie with becoming a GM-free community or local body. For example, it is argued that GM-free communities would be liable if "an easily controlled bug that is breeding out of control in a GM-free area" ravaged GM farmers' crops (Life Sciences Network, 2002c, p. 6). Thus, environmental risk is *rearticulated* with GM-free zones and *disarticulated* from GM itself.

Having established the difficulties and disadvantages of becoming GM-free, the information kit then reassures readers of the safety of GM foods. It does this using a very simple explanation of the fact that all foods contain genes. In inviting readers to consider the issues of eating GM foods that *combine* plant and animal genes, the information kit stated that "it is not dangerous to eat the genes from plants and animals together ... . If you eat a meal of meat and vegetables you are eating the genes of plants and animals together" (Life Sciences Network, 2002c, p. 12). Thus, risk is neutralized by articulating transgenic engineering with the meals that we already eat and by extracting the complex scientific processes of GM from the discursive explanation of the effects of eating GM foods.

As our discourse analysis of the Life Sciences Network campaign has demonstrated, the strategic use of discourse is central to public relations practice and solicitation of public consent to pursue an organizational mission. The first Life Sciences Network advertorial drew on a risk discourse strategy to accentuate the safety of GM and thereby minimize and counter the opposing anti-GM discursive strategy emphasizing environmental and health risks. Within the second advertorial, risk again featured, this time as a strategy to emphasize the economic risks of rejecting GM science. Thus, the GM debate was articulated to the dominant political economy discourse. Within the Internet-based information kit, the discursive strategy highlighted the economic and social risks of establishing a GM-free zone. The use of experts, an environmental activist and a woman scientist, served to create doubts about the uncertainties and criticisms of GM. The audience was not offered an open choice of what discourse to prefer—the struggle to achieve hegemony was underpinned by a strategy of positioning the pro-GM discourse as *the truth*: The Life Sciences Network had the "facts," therefore, anti-GM discourses could not maintain their "regime of truth."

From a critical discourse perspective the Life Sciences Network campaign is interpreted as positioning a pro-GM stance as a win–win position for the Life Sciences Network clients and in the interest of the New Zealand public. Consequently, the notion of "the public interest" can be understood as a contestable discursive construction that may be deployed to influence public opinion and policy. To articulate the public relations campaign as representing the public interest, the message communicated was framed in terms of the political economy agenda. The campaign did not function as a public education campaign that developed New Zealanders' understanding of GM science or advanced the GM debate, but instead used public funding during an election to overtly promote a particular political and economic ideological agenda in relation to GM. Interestingly, although we are not entirely attributing the election outcome to the Life Sciences Network campaign, in the 2002 national government election the Green and Alliance parties, and the anti-GM lobby, experienced a significant decline in public support, and they lost several of their key constituency Members of Parliament.

CONCLUSIONS

In applying political economy and discourse analysis to the critical study of public relations we have demonstrated the value of researching and theorizing the social and political implications of communication practice. Our analysis of the Life Sciences Network campaign illustrated how public relations deploys discourse strategies to promote, maintain, and resist dominant political and economic ideologies. The issue of GM was disarticulated from the scientific and environmental discourse domains and rearticulated as an economic discourse in order to align GM with the "superordinate" agenda of mainstream New Zealand politics. In this way, the campaign took an undeclared political stance to support particular political agendas. From this perspective, it can be seen how a political economy analysis informs critical discourse analysis by way of explicitly identifying the sociopolitical contexts in which public relations operates and which it seeks to influence.

Analysis of the campaign discourse demonstrated the way that the Life Sciences Network sought to disqualify anti-GM discourses and knowledge and sanction pro-GM knowledge. The example of the Life Sciences Network advertorial campaign demonstrates how public relations participates in a discursive struggle to establish the status of truth because, from a critical theory perspective, truth is understood as contingent and relative. Our critical analysis of the campaign also illustrates the strategies through which groups can attempt to gain public consent to pursue their organizational mission. It identified how win–win scenarios can articulate organizational interest with public interest in a specific historical sociopolitical context, and how that context itself determines the way "the public interest" is defined.

Discourse analysis offers critical scholars a mode for researching and theorizing the public relations practices that structure societal systems of knowledge and beliefs, the rules that are being established to shape or challenge the way we construct our thinking, and the role of public relations in influencing social change in democratic societies. A limitation of using discourse analysis alone is that it may neglect reference to real practice (Mills, 1997; Philo & Miller, 2001), a weakness that an integrated political economy and discourse analysis seek to overcome. The challenge for critical public relations researchers is to place the issues of power and truth at the center of their inquiry in order to more fully understand the role of public relations in democratic decision making processes.

REFERENCES

Allen, T. (2000). The environmental costs of genetic engineering. In R. Prebble (Ed.), *Designer genes: The New Zealand guide to the issues, facts and theories about genetic engineering* (pp. 61–68). Wellington, New Zealand: Dark Horse.

Beck, U. (2000). Foreword. In S. Allen, B. Adam, & C. Carter (Eds.), *Environmental risks and the media* (pp. xii–xiv). London: Routledge.

Berger, B. K. (2005/this issue). Power over, power with, and power to relations: Critical reflections on public relations, the dominant coalition, and activism. *Journal of Public Relations Research, 17,* 5–27.

Bruno, K. (1998). Monsanto's failing PR strategy. *The Ecologist, 28,* 287–93.

Clark, L. (2002, July 25). Interview with Jeanette Fitzsimons and Peter Hodgson on the Life Sciences Network advertorial campaign [Radio interview]. *Morning till noon.* Wellington, New Zealand: Radio New Zealand.

Collins, S. (2002a, July 25). Taxpayer cash in pro-GM adverts. *The New Zealand Herald,* p. 1.

Collins, S. (2002b, July 26). Varsity unit gives cash to pro-GM fund. *The New Zealand Herald,* p. 4.

Conner, T. (2000). Crops, food, environment and ethics. In R. Prebble (Ed.), *Designer genes: The New Zealand guide to the issues, facts and theories about genetic engineering* (pp. 141–151). Wellington, New Zealand: Dark Horse.

Downing, J., Mohammadi, A., & Sreberny-Mohammadi, A. (1995). Preface. In J. Downing, A. Mohammadi, & A. Sreberny-Mohammadi (Eds.), *Questioning the media: A critical introduction* (pp. xv–xxix). Thousand Oaks, CA: Sage.

Dozier, D. M., Grunig, L. A., & Grunig, J. E. (1995). *Managers guide to excellence in public relations and communication management.* Mahwah, NJ: Lawrence Erlbaum Associates, Inc.

Durham, F. (2005/this issue). Public relations as structuration: A prescriptive critique of the StarLink global food contamination case. *Journal of Public Relations Research, 17,* 29–47.

Fairclough, N. (1992). *Discourse and social change.* Oxford: Polity.

Fitzsimons, J. (2000). The nuclear-free issue of the 21st century. In R. Prebble (Ed.), *Designer genes: The New Zealand guide to the issues, facts and theories about genetic engineering* (pp. 187–196). Wellington, New Zealand: Dark Horse.

Foucault, M. (1972). *The archaeology of knowledge.* London: Routledge.

Foucault, M. (1980). *Power/knowledge: Selected interviews and other writings 1972–1977.* New York: Pantheon.

Foucault, M. (1996). *Foucault live (Interviews 1966–1984)* (S. Lotringer, Ed.; J. Johnston, Trans.). New York: Semiotext(e).

Garnham N. (1997). Political economy and the practice of cultural studies. In M. Ferguson & P. Golding (Eds.), *Cultural studies in question* (pp. 56–73). London: Sage.

Golding, M., & Murdock, G. (1991). Culture, communications, and political economy. In J. Curran & M. Gurevitch (Eds.), *Mass media and society* (pp.15–32). London: Arnold.

Grunig, J. E. (2001). Two-way symmetrical public relations: Past, present and future. In R. L. Heath (Ed.), *Handbook of public relations* (pp. 11–30). London: Sage.

Hager, N. (2002). *Seeds of distrust*. Nelson, New Zealand: Potten.

Hall, S. (1986). On postmodernism and articulation. *Journal of Communication Inquiry, 10*(2), 45–60.

Ho, M.-W. (1999). *Genetic engineering: Dream or nightmare?* Dublin, Ireland: Gateway.

Holtzhausen, D. R. (2000). Postmodern values in public relations. *Journal of Public Relations Research, 12,* 93–114.

Jesson, B. (1999). *Only their purpose is mad: The money men take over NZ.* Palmerston North, New Zealand: Dunmore.

Kelsey, J. (1997). *The New Zealand experiment: A world model for structural adjustment* (2nd ed.). Auckland, New Zealand: Auckland University Press.

Kelsey, J. (2002). *At the crossroads: Three essays*. Wellington, New Zealand: Williams.

Kettle, P. (2000). Do genes have a sense of belonging? In R. Prebble (Ed.), *Designer genes: The New Zealand guide to the issues, facts and theories about genetic engineering* (pp. 153–162). Wellington, New Zealand: Dark Horse.

L'Etang, J., & Pieczka, M. (Eds.). (1996). *Critical perspectives in public relations*. London: International Thomson.

Life Sciences Network. (2002a). *Archives*. Retrieved July 18, 2002, from http://www.lifesciencesnetwork.com/educationarchives.asp

Life Sciences Network. (2002b). *The constitution of the Life Sciences Network Incorporated*. Retrieved July 26, 2002, from http://www.lifesciencesnetwork.com/repository/LSNConstitution.pdf

Life Sciences Network. (2002c). *GM—The public's right to choose. An information kit prepared by the Life Sciences Network.* Retrieved July 26, 2002, from http://www.lifesciencesnetwork.com/repository/020523_LocalBodies.pdf

Life Sciences Network. (2002d, June 22). In the GE debate, the facts have been modified beyond recognition [Advertorial]. *The New Zealand Herald*, p. 8.

Life Sciences Network. (2002e, June 22). The only thing about the approved use of GM technology that will make you sick is the misinformation surrounding the debate [Advertorial]. *Waikato Times*, p. 22.

McKie, D. (2001). Updating public relations: "New science," research paradigms, and uneven developments. In R. L. Heath (Ed.), *Handbook of public relations* (pp. 75–91). Thousand Oaks, CA: Sage.

Mickey, T. J. (1998). Selling the Internet: A cultural studies approach to public relations. *Public Relations Review, 24,* 335–349.

Miller, D., & Dinan, W. (2000). The rise of the PR industry in Britain, 1979–98. *European Journal of Communication, 15*(1), 5–35.

Mills, S. (1997). *Discourse*. London: Routledge.

Ministry for the Environment. (2004). *HSNO: Hazardous substances and new organisms*. Retrieved November 2, 2004, from http://www.hsno.govt.nz

Moffit, M. A. (1994). Collapsing and integrating concepts of "public" and "image" into a new theory. *Public Relations Review, 20,* 159–170.

Mosco, V. (1996). *The political economy of communication*. London: Sage.

Motion, J., & Leitch, S. (1996). A discursive perspective from New Zealand: Another world view. *Public Relations Review, 22,* 297–309.

Motion, J., & Leitch, S. (2001). New Zealand perspectives on public relations. In R. L. Heath (Ed.), *Handbook of public relations* (pp. 659–663). Thousand Oaks, CA: Sage.

Philo, G., & Miller, D. (2000). Cultural compliance and critical media studies. *Media Culture and Society, 22,* 831–839.

Philo, G., & Miller, D. (2001) Cultural compliance: Media/cultural studies and social science. In G. Philo & D. Miller (Eds.), *Market killing: What the free market does and what social scientists can do about it* (pp. 3–95). Harlow, England: Longman.

Roper, J. (2005/this issue). Symmetrical communication: Excellent public relations or a strategy for hegemony? *Journal of Public Relations Research, 17,* 69–86.

Royal Commission on Genetic Modification. (2001). Executive summary. Retrieved August 7, 2002, from http://www.gmcommission.govt.nz/RCGM/pdfs/report/execSumm.pdf

Switzer, L., McNamara, J., & Ryan, M. (1999). Critical-cultural studies in research and instruction, *Journalism and Mass Communication Educator, 54*(3), 23–42.

Trujillo, N., & Toth, E. L. (1987). Organizational perspectives for public relations research and practice. *Management Communication Quarterly, 1,* 199–231.

Weaver, C. K., & Motion, J. (2002). Sabotage and subterfuge: Public relations, democracy and genetic engineering in New Zealand. *Media, Culture & Society, 24,* 325–343.

Weaver, C. K. (2001) Dressing for battle in the new global economy: Putting power, identity, and discourse into public relations theory. *Management Communication Quarterly, 15,* 279–288.

JOURNAL OF PUBLIC RELATIONS RESEARCH, *17*(1), 69–86
Copyright © 2005, Lawrence Erlbaum Associates, Inc.

Symmetrical Communication: Excellent Public Relations or a Strategy for Hegemony?

Juliet Roper

Department of Management Communication
University of Waikato

This article examines the process of symmetrical communication, as described by J. E. Grunig, through the critical lens of the concept of hegemony. The practice of symmetrical communication is commonly considered to be the model for excellent and ethical public relations. However, this article questions the ethics of a process that is often one of compromise to deflect criticism and maintain power relations rather than one of open, collaborative negotiation.

Two-way symmetrical communication, as conceptualized by James E. Grunig, is said to form the basis of excellent public relations practice. From this perspective, symmetrical communication is characterized by a willingness of an organization to listen and respond to the concerns and interests of its key stakeholders: "Excellent organizations 'stay close' to their customers, employees, and other *strategic constituencies*" (J. E. Grunig, 1992, p. 16). What is key here is that the response of the organization will be a substantive one, not just a discursive shift. At the other end of the spectrum of public relations practice lies what J. E. Grunig termed *two-way asymmetrical communication,* whereby organizations listen to their stakeholders but use the information thus obtained to tailor their communication to allay the concerns of stakeholders, but do not make a corresponding alteration to their behavior.

In a later reflection of his four-part model of public relations, J. E. Grunig (2001) aligned Murphy's (1991) description of a mixed-motive model with his own original conceptualization of the symmetrical model. That is, he acknowl-

---

Requests for reprints should be sent to Juliet Roper, Department of Management Communication, University of Waikato, Private Bag 3105, Hamilton, New Zealand. Email: jroper@waikato.ac.nz

edged that it is to be expected that any organization that practices symmetrical communication is doing so in order to satisfy their own interests as well as those of their publics. This would imply mutual satisfaction rather than sacrifice on the part of one party.

These perspectives hold if the discussion fails to critically appraise what underlies the words *motive* and *interests*. If these are the words that are to be associated with *excellence* then one would assume equality in the negotiating of mutual interest. Questions of (in)equality at the "negotiating table" already have been addressed by other critical scholars of public relations, usually in terms of resources and negotiating power (see, e.g, Cheney & Christensen, 2001; Leitch & Neilson, 2001). The notion of symmetrical communication also has been compared with the Habermasian (1987) concept of communicative action, based on the principles of the public sphere where self interest is put aside in favor of the "public good" (see Leitch & Neilson, 2001).

This article explores the application of another concept, fundamental to critical theory and widely used in cultural studies, which offers a further perspective on the way in which symmetrical public relations can be seen to operate. That concept is hegemony (Gramsci, 1971; Hall, 1988a).

Hegemony can be defined as domination without physical coercion through the widespread acceptance of particular ideologies and consent to the practices associated with those ideologies. Hegemony includes the notion of "moral and philosophical leadership" (Bocock, 1986, p. 11) but the acceptance of that leadership is not achieved through recognized democratic processes of open debate of alternative positions. Rather, it is achieved and maintained through the manufacturing of consent (Fairclough, 1992). In Bocock's (1986) words, "for Gramsci hegemonic leadership fundamentally involved producing a world-view, a philosophy and moral outlook, which other subordinate and allied classes, and groups, in a society accepted" (p. 46). According to Gramsci (1971), power, which is the product of consent, is not only exercised in the realm of the economic sphere but also in the spheres of the state and civil society, and it is specifically in these realms that hegemony was created and maintained (Holub, 1992).

This understanding of the nature of hegemony, importantly for this article, does not suggest that ideas can be imposed on passive publics who will not question their basis. Hegemony is constantly challenged at multiple sites for multiple reasons, and the only way it can be maintained is through the making of concessions at key areas of contestation. As Stuart Hall (1988a) put it, hegemony implies

> the struggle to contest and dis-organize an existing political formation; the taking of the "leading position" (on however a minority basis) over a number of different spheres of society at once—economy, civil society, intellectual and moral life, culture; the conduct of a wide and differentiated type of struggle; the winning of a strategic measure of popular consent; and, thus, the securing of a social authority suffi-

ciently deep to conform society into a new historical project. It should never be taken for a finished or settled project. It is always contested, always trying to secure itself, always "in process." (p. 7)

If concessions in response to opposition were not made and dominant practices instead remained static, resistance would grow to the point where stability would be lost. Thus practices of dominant organizations must be dynamic or be stalled by overwhelming opposition. Levy (1997, 2001) applied this important realization to the discipline of strategic management. As public relations practitioners continue to argue for the inclusion of a public relations perspective within management at a strategic level, it is both relevant and appropriate that the concept of hegemony also be considered within public relations theory and practice.

As stated previously, hegemony involves domination throughout all spheres of society. Thus within democratic nations and, increasingly, internationally, it is contested and maintained by power struggles within and between the major power blocs of society: the state, the economy, and civil society. According to Cohen and Arato (1992), who drew heavily on the theory of Jurgen Habermas, civil society comprises "the intimate sphere (especially the family); the sphere of associations (in particular, voluntary associations); social movements, and forms of public communication" (p. ix).

More important, Habermas's (1979, 1991) notion of civil society is grounded in democratic theory and, as such, is antithetical to the concept of hegemony and the manipulation of power relations. However, Habermas (1987, 1991, 1992, 1996), along with others of the Frankfurt School, drew on Marxist theory, as did Gramsci, although the commonality is not acknowledged. In particular, Habermas's theory of communicative action (Habermas, 1987, 1996) and the public sphere (Habermas, 1991, 1992) were developed as a basis for critique of the current state of Western democratic nations. Habermas (1991, 1992) identified the public sphere as the public realm of civil society, which is concerned with issues of politics, but also as a realm distinguished by open discourse between individuals, with personal interests set aside, that allows for the rational formation of public opinion. The necessary basis of communicative action is that dialogue is free of strategic intent, and, as a consequence, resulting public opinion is collaboratively negotiated. Within the realm of the state are included public organizations such as elected governments (local, national, or international), other (opposition) political parties or individuals elected to office, government agents such as public service institutions, and the judiciary, which executes the laws of the state although, ideally, it does so independently of state influence. The economy comprises those private organizations whose primary reason for existence is economic. Thus it would include large corporations and small businesses. By virtue of their large size and consequent potential for influence, corporations, rather than small businesses, are the focus of discussion of the economy here.

This article examines the role of communication (through public relations) in and the nature of the power struggles and negotiated alliances between the institutions of the state (primarily government) and those of the economy. It then goes on to examine the ways in which these dominant power centers are challenged by activists of civil society and the efforts made to undermine the power of these disruptive challenges. Central to and implicit in the discussion is the role of negotiation and concession as a strategy for hegemony.

PATHWAYS OF COMMUNICATION, NEGOTIATION, AND INFLUENCE

The divisions between the state, the economy, and civil society are by no means distinct and are constantly being challenged and negotiated. Under market driven capitalism, for example, the pathways of influence between civil society and the economy are less distinct because of the ways in which the two have necessarily become intertwined (Dahlgren, 1995). Hospitals and schools provide interesting examples. Under systems of social democracy these institutions are traditionally funded by the state but in practice operate within civil society with varying degrees of policy direction from the state. Their ultimate role will depend on the conditions under which the funding was provided. With the introduction of the "user pays," free market philosophy of laissez-faire neo-liberalism and its associated reduction in state funding, the operation of hospitals and schools is increasingly removed from civil society and placed within the economy, dependent on selling services for survival.

The directions and nature of the pathways of communication between the state, the economy, and civil society can serve to highlight power relationships and strategies of influence. Ultimately, it is the state that is pivotal in pathways of communication and influence as negotiations of power are overwhelmingly associated with public policy, the domain of the state. This fundamental assumption is reflected in Heath's (1997) conception of organizational issues management as designed to prevent the introduction or mitigate the effects of unfavorable public policy. Organizations of the economy may negotiate (through lobbying) issues of policy directly with the state, or they may exercise issues management by negotiation with civil society in order to forestall demands for regulation. However, if negotiations are conducted between the state and the economy, policy outcomes will eventually require legitimation from civil society, as described later in this article.

The nature and directions of the pathways of policy negotiations also can serve as indicators of social and political change as the balance of power shifts over time. This is particularly evident in the discourses employed by key protagonists as the discourses both seek to shape and construct relationships and are, in turn, shaped by those relationships (see Fairclough, 1989, 1992). The shifts in relative dominance of power in policy negotiations between the economy, the state, and civil society will be reflected in the discourses of negotiation where deference will be paid according to whom is perceived as more influential. In many instances the construction of discourse that seeks to influence negotiated outcomes is effected by public relations professionals (see Motion & Leitch, 1996). In this article, I am concerned with the ways in which the different forms of asymmetrical and symmetrical communication, as described by J. E. Grunig and Hunt (1984), are employed in policy negotiations and, more important, the extent to which the application of symmetrical communication can be said to embody excellence in public relations.

CONTEXTUALIZING POLICY NEGOTIATIONS

Negotiations of power relationships and policy formation do not occur in isolation from any of the key blocs of society previously identified, but, rather, they are sensitive to social norms at any given time and place. Thus it is important to contextualize any discussion of power shifts within a historical context. Throughout the modern history of capitalist, democratic regimes there has been an uneasy tension between the state, the economy, and civil society. With shifts in dominant ideologies, there also have been shifts in the nature of the relationship between these power blocs. For example, during the post-World War II period of Keynesian social democracy, the power of governments to control their national economies through means such as tariffs and subsidies, and their simultaneous responsibility to provide for the welfare of citizens through, for example, state-funded education, health, and superannuation, were unquestioned. Their power and their relationship with civil society were hegemonic by virtue of acceptance of their social and economic policies as common sense. Public opinion would not allow the introduction of policies that favored the economy over civil society.

That hegemony began to disintegrate in the 1970s as the basis of the Keynesian economic model was called into question. By the 1980s Keynesian social democracy had been replaced in many democracies around the world by the free market ideologies of laissez-faire neoliberalism. With that change came a shift in the relationships between state and economy, with the direct role of the state being altered, in some cases through the privatization of state-owned enterprises such as electric companies or, in others, through a shift toward a market model for the provision of public services such as medical care and education. In either way, the result was in favor of the power of the economy to control its own policies and practices and to take a much greater role in the social sector. Governments were not passive in the power shift but took an active role in it. As Burchell (1996) put it:

> Governments must work for the game of market competition and as a kind of enterprise itself, and new quasi-entrepreneurial and market models of action or practical systems must be invented for the conduct of individuals, groups and institutions

within those areas of life hitherto seen as being either outside of or even antagonistic to the economic. (p. 27)

The shift in policies away from national government regulation of the economic sector facilitated corporate mergers on a global scale, resulting in the first truly transnational enterprises (Kuttner, 2000). Then, once the deregulation of policies was extended to include trading in capital and securities markets in 1987, capital began to flow freely around the world, as traders sought to maximize the value of their investments, and a global economy was introduced (Castells, 2000, p. 53). Movement of capital on a global scale grew exponentially from then on. Castells cited a 1998 average daily rate of currency exchange on global markets as the equivalent of US $1.5 trillion, representing an 800% increase from 1986 to 1998 (p. 55).

A key element in the creation of a global economy has been the development of new information and communication technologies. Powerful computers, networking software, organizational software, and electronic exchange systems have combined to enable virtually instant financial transactions to take place around the world, regardless of time zones. These developments have precipitated a major shift in the balance of power between the state and the economy as the speed, unpredictability, and volatility of capital movement have resulted in a global financial market that is "beyond the control of governments, financial institutions and specific business groups—regardless of their size and wealth" (Castells, 2000, p. 59).

The neo-liberal approach to global free markets has ultimately placed corporations in a position of power over both the state (particularly in Third World nations) and the citizens of civil society, with national governments favoring the economic sector over civil society in policy decisions. As Grossman (1998) put it,

> Politicians say, "We have to create a good business climate. We have to give the corporations whatever they want, including all kinds of subsidies and special privileges" .... It's quite clear that today the corporations, corporate values, corporate money control political debate in this country [USA]. They control our legislatures as well as the courts. They control the press and have a dominant effect upon education, whether it's kindergarten, high school or the universities. (cited in Barsamian, 1998, ¶8)

As neoliberal policies have encountered increasing criticism in the face of evidence of their being responsible for growing extremes of wealth and poverty, unemployment and environmental damage, there has been a further, although often subtle, shift in relative power among the state, the economy, and civil society. Because groups within the political arena always need to remain alert to shifts in public perceptions and opinion, many Western political parties, notably Clinton's Democrats of the United States and Blair's New Labour of the United Kingdom, have adopted and been elected to government on the basis of their Third Way Policies, as theorized by Giddens (1998, 2000). These policies are said to bridge the divide between social concerns and support for a market economy although the extent to which they do so in practice varies from nation to nation. Essentially, these governments recognize value in a global economy and free trade but they also recognize a need for a more active, less market driven role of the state in provision of social welfare such as health and education.

There is, however, a limit to the degree to which power shifts in democratic societies and associated policy changes can be effected. The power relationship between the state and the economy, as described previously by Grossman (1998), cannot be maintained without reference to other power blocs of society because no matter how relations between the state and the economy are negotiated and whatever the outcomes, from the perspective of democratic theory both the process and the results ultimately require support from civil society in the form of legitimation (Habermas, 1976, 1996). Legitimation, according to Habermas, is provided by civil society for institutions of the political sphere when their policies and actions are considered to be rational because they coincide with existing social norms. The same applies to policies of institutions of the economy when they affect civil society. Ideally, public opinion, which establishes social norms, is formed through open discussion within the public sphere of civil society and is based on full information regarding issues of public importance (Habermas, 1979). This view is, as discussed previously, counter to the notion of hegemony, which implies the strategic manipulation of public opinion. Habermas did, however, allow for contingencies through which the dominant power blocs of the state (or the economy) can compensate for a lack of policy rationality. Compensation can be made by the provision of material or "consumable values" (Habermas, 1976, p. 93) such as those provided by welfare state programs. The greater the lack of rationality, the greater the demand for compensation and the greater the revenue required by governments for public spending. If the economic sector fails to generate sufficient revenue for the state, through, for example, taxation, then public spending will be withdrawn, along with legitimation. An inability to afford material compensation for irrational policy would result in both economic and legitimation crises for the state (Habermas, 1976).

With the economy in a position to remove its capital readily from one nation to another, governments of nation states find themselves increasingly obliged to create and protect an infrastructure that favors corporations and the financial institutions that support them. That imperative is supported by multilateral economic institutions, such as the World Trade Organization (WTO), the International Monetary Fund (IMF), and the World Bank, that work together in an attempt to bind national governments to policies of deregulation and a focus on production for export and the earning of foreign exchange, often at the expense of their own citizens' welfare (O'Brien, Goetz, Scholte, & Williams, 2000). Thus, as also suggested previously by Grossman, the political power and influence of global corporations has grown "at the expense of nation-states that once balanced their private economic power with public purposes and national stabilization policies" (Kuttner, 2000, p. 147).

Despite the more recent development of coercive power of corporations through the agency of WTO, IMF, and World Bank policies, however, power relations between the major blocs still can be shifted. Indeed, if that were not the case serious issues regarding the nature of modern democracies would be (and are) raised. Unless they are completely destabilized by economic and legitimation crises, governments of nation states retain sufficient power to introduce policy shifts designed to curb the power of the economy over other sectors of society. Increasingly, as dissent grows and public spheres move from being passive to active (Habermas, 1996), there is demand from civil society, both at a national and international level, for them to do so. Within their own countries, governments face the prospect of being voted out of office at the next election if they fail to respond to that demand. Internationally, there is widespread protest against the collective globalization policies of the WTO, the World Bank, and the IMF. These protests are on the grounds of environmental issues, labor issues, and concerns of national identity, among others. Governments must respond to the concerns of the protesters as they become increasingly powerful in terms of numbers, skill (through training and technology), and organization (Roper, 2002). Corporations must also respond to the protesters if they are to exercise issues management and prevent the introduction of substantive policy changes that they perceive to be counter to corporate interests.

Within democratic nations, it is to be expected, coercion is not a viable option. Coercion certainly has been used in an attempt to quell the protests against globalization that have been held in Seattle and Genoa, among others. However, coercion will not help persuade citizens that policies under question are in their best interests. Communication is what is required and managing that communication is the role of public relations professionals. All four forms of communication identified by J. E. Grunig and Hunt (1984; press agentry, public information, two-way asymmetrical, and two-way symmetrical communication) are reported as employed by governments and corporations in their attempts to manage their relationships with each other and with civil society, as explored next. The key question asked in this article is whether the objective of their relationship management is to maintain an environment that enables organizations (business or government) to meet their own policy objectives or whether it entails a collaborative negotiation of the policy objectives themselves.

Asymmetrical Communication

The nature of communication within and among the state, the economy, and civil society often can be regarded as discursive attempts to shape perceptions in which case the communication falls into the asymmetrical category. Very often, debate is over the discursive construction of what constitutes the "public interest" or "public good" (Gallhofer, Haslam, & Roper, 2001; see also Motion & Weaver, 2005/this issue) because, ultimately that is what will be consented to by civil society, by whatever means, strategic or democratic. The vehicle of the struggle is discourse. As Fairclough (1995) explained, "The power to control discourse is seen as the power to sustain particular discursive practices with particular ideological investments in dominance over other alternative (including oppositional) practices" (p. 2). The hegemonic struggle is for the establishment of "common knowledge," for when knowledge becomes common sense it will cease to be questioned (Hall, 1988a).

Hegemony is never permanent. It is constantly challenged at multiple sites by contradictory and opposing interests at every level of society (Eley, 1992; Fairclough, 1992; Hall, 1988b). The pathways of influence within and between the potential power blocs of society can be complex and multidirectional. For example, it is often the case that economically powerful institutions will sponsor research from academics in the private sphere in order to support their arguments with the State, which may not have the resources to undergo its own research. Gandy (1992) referred to such sponsored research as information subsidies and maintained that "policy actors provide indirect subsidies through a variety of means, most of which have to do with using a credible source to deliver a persuasive message" (p. 143). Business groups also have been known to have paid academics to act as independent referees for business sponsored reports, presumably in direct response to the criticisms leveled at the use of sponsored research to further political and economic interests.

Governments and politicians seeking office typically (although not exclusively) will employ asymmetrical communication, most notably during election campaigns. They employ political communicators who conduct their own audience research, particularly in the pretesting of messages, before they are incorporated into political campaigns (Maarek, 1995; Newman, 1994) to be disseminated by the media. This "scientificization" (Habermas, 1974; Mancini & Swanson, 1996) or "technologization" (Fairclough, 1995) of discourse raises concerns regarding the breakdown of traditional arenas and functions of public discourse as, according to Mayhew (1997), message pretesting can serve to "remove the shaping of public debate from the public arena and locate it instead in the research designs of professional political experts" (p. 215). By privately simulating discussions that might otherwise occur publicly, market research can allow the avoidance of "unanticipated negative responses or reinterpretations of carefully planned campaign messages" (p. 216).

None of these described instances of communicative influence suggests a substantive response on the part of the communicator. Rather, the emphasis is either on persuading any potential opposition that a particular policy direction is in the interests of society, or the discourse is tailored to articulate with (Hall, 1986; Motion & Leitch, 1996) the expectations of its target public. By virtue of a lack of willingness to alter practices in order to meet the needs of particular publics, or those of broader society, J. E. Grunig (2001) concluded that asymmetrical communication does not concur with best practice of public relations.

Symmetrical Communication

When discourse alone is insufficient to persuade key publics of the rationality of public policy or of business practices, asymmetrical communication will fail to establish the stable environment that is the objective of public relations. With growing cynicism within civil society, persuasive arguments from those in power, particularly economic power, are often met with mistrust. For example, as cynicism has grown regarding corporate claims of environmental responsibility, dissenting publics have introduced the term *greenwash* (Beder, 1997) to indicate a lack of substance to the corporate claims.

As the power and confidence of the public sphere grows, so too do demands for substantive reconfigurations of policy and behavior by actors of the state and the economy. As previously stated, if public policy is not seen as rational or is not substantively compensated for, legitimacy will be withdrawn from the state to such an extent that governments will be forced to reprioritize and renegotiate their relationships with civil society, even at the expense of relationships with the economy. Symmetrical communication, according to J. E. Grunig and Hunt (1984), included a substantive response in the form of a shift in practice to match the discourse.

Responses by organizations within the realms of the state and the economy to the demands and concerns of dissenting groups of the public sphere are made by individual governments and by groups, notably corporations, of the economy. This section explores some examples of these responses that could be said to fit within the category of symmetrical communication.

The WTO, the World Bank, and the IMF.   Although the World Trade Organization (WTO) is an international regulatory body, or a multilateral economic institution (MEI; O'Brien et al., 2000) that has the active support of governments, especially those of wealthy Western nations that established it, it is generally considered to act on behalf of the economy because of its agenda of expanding and enforcing global economic policies. Large multinational corporations are widely considered to be the key beneficiaries of these policies as well as the direct causes of environmental and labor problems associated with globalization. As previously stated, the WTO's policies are supported by those of two other MEIs, the World Bank and the IMF, through their policies of structural adjustment that are designed primarily to open developing nations to international free trade. All three of these organizations are subject to protests by groups in the public sphere, and all three claim to have made substantive responses to protesters' concerns.

The World Bank is the most sensitive of the three MEIs to social movements because of its vulnerability to specific project interference by protesters. Also, the Bank relies on the U.S. government for its financing and the U.S. government in turn, like other elected governments, is reliant on the support of public opinion. Thus the World Bank must be seen to be responsive to public opinion in the form of social movements of the public sphere (see O'Brien et al., 2000). As a part of that response, the Bank has formally replaced its structural adjustment policies with a new "Comprehensive Development Framework" (Bello, 2000). It also has moved to include social movements and nongovernmental organizations (NGOs) in policy discussions. O'Brien et al. discussed specifically the changes made within the World Bank to build its relationships with environmental NGOs and women's groups.

Like the World Bank, the IMF is dependent on member states for its funding and so must also be seen to be responsive to social concerns. Although its contact with social movements and NGOs has not been as extensive as that of the World Bank, that contact is growing with a key focus on organized labor groups (O'Brien et al., 2000). The WTO also has recently opened itself up to involvement with NGOs in response to demands for a more open and inclusive decision making process. This organization's inclusion of NGOs in discussions of policy has been on selected issues and there is some consultation in dispute settlement (O'Brien et al., 2000). The greatest challenge to international business, however, is the emergence of environmental issues on a global scale which "have presented business with the threat of coordinated international action that could cause serious disruption to markets" (Levy, 1997, p. 130). That coordinated action is through the establishment of Multilateral Environmental Agreements, such as the Kyoto Protocol, which have policies that, in many instances, run counter to the policies of the WTO (Chambers, 2001).

Shell.   Many NGOs of civil society consider it much more effective to directly target corporations to bring about reform than to target the WTO itself or national governments. Thus we see a shift in traditional pathways of power negotiations to exclude the state and to operate instead between the economy and the public sphere (see, e.g., Klein, 1999; Newell, 2000). The public sphere, however, cannot legislatively enforce compliance with its interests. That remains the domain of the state.

Whether it is in response to the direct protests or negotiations of NGOs of the public sphere or to the possibility of public opinion forcing the state to take legislative action, individual corporations must listen and respond substantively to public dissent. The case of Royal Dutch/Shell provides an example of a multinational corporation that is a key target of direct protests (Yearley & Forrester, 2000). It is also an example of a corporation that benefits from WTO, World Bank, and IMF policies while at the same time stands to be affected by the challenge to those policies by Multilateral Environmental Agreements, particularly the Kyoto Protocol (Chambers, 2001).

For Shell, the realization that the corporation had to be more responsive to its broad range of stakeholders came after two events, both in 1995, which amounted to public relations disasters for Shell. The first, the Brent Spar controversy, centered on the proposed disposal of an obsolete oil-storage platform by sinking it in the Atlantic Ocean off the coast of Scotland, a move that was vigorously opposed by Greenpeace. Part of the Greenpeace-led campaign was a very successful consumer boycott of Shell products, which had the potential to directly impact on the viability of the company. The second case centered on Shell's disregard for the welfare of the local people and the environment during its decades of operations in Nigeria. During that time the company faced repeated protests by the local people but the incident that fueled world wide controversy was the Nigerian Government's execution of the activist leader of the Ogoni Tribe, Ken Saro-Wiwa. It was widely believed that the execution could have been prevented if Shell had intervened instead of refusing to do so (for a fuller explanation of these cases see, e.g., Livesey, 2001; Yearley & Forrester, 2000).

These events made Shell closely examine both its public perception and its performance in the areas of environmental and social sustainability. In response Shell undertook a commitment to the principles of sustainability, with a review of its operations. In putting together its first sustainability "triple bottom line" (Elkington, 1999) report, "Profits and Principles," Shell brought in John Elkington, the originator of the concept, as a consultant (Livesey, 2001). Elkington's involvement lent credibility and authority to the report itself and, by extrapolation, to Shell. The report, through statements such as, "This report is part of a dialogue, and we will continue to seek your views" (Knight, 1998, p. 1), was clearly set up to demonstrate Shell's shift to a two-way symmetrical form of public relations.

Shell's public relations efforts arguably have been successful in turning public perception of the company around to a more favorable view. Not only has Shell sought the views of its stakeholders, including environmentalists, but it also has altered its behavior. The degree of its commitment to respond substantively to the environmental and social concerns of civil society, however, remains under question.

The greatest challenge faced today by Shell, along with all other major oil companies, is that of climate change. The realization that carbon emissions are largely responsible for the warming of the Earth and its atmosphere has fundamental implications for the oil industry because "it threatens its primary businesses of oil exploration and production; its authority to participate in policy making; and its right to control and profit from natural resources" (Livesey & Shearer, 2003, p. 1). In response to the issue of climate change, Shell continues to publicly position itself as a company guided by the principles of sustainability, according equal importance to social, environmental, and economic factors of the company's performance. In

1998 it followed BP[1] in leaving the Global Climate Change Coalition, a powerful United States based lobby group against compulsory measures to mitigate greenhouse gases (Brown, 2000; Leggett, 1999) and joined the Pew Center on Global Climate Change. Members of this new organization publicly stated, through a series of advertisements, that they "accept the views of most scientists that enough is known about the science and environmental impacts of climate change for us to take actions to address its consequences" (Levy, 2001, p. 21).

Shell's public endorsement of these views represents a shift in the company's attitude and public relations. In support of its statements, Shell also has made substantive shifts in practice, reducing its own greenhouse gas emissions and pledging to invest $100 million a year in renewable energy sources and a further $500 million over 5 years in photovoltaics. Yet, serious questions remain regarding the extent of these shifts. Its $100 million investment represents "only about 7% of the company's total annual expenditure on petroleum exploration and production" (Levy, 2001, p. 21). The company continues to expand its oil exploration and production divisions, including by way of a World Bank funded oil pipeline through Central African rainforests (Yearley & Forrester, 2000).

In New Zealand, Shell was one of a large number of industries that sought to influence public policy decisions by making submissions to the government against ratification of the Kyoto Protocol on the grounds that Shell (and New Zealand) would be put at a competitive (and thus economic) disadvantage (Roper & Collins, 2003). In its submission as a part of the New Zealand Government's first consultation round ("Consultation Round One Submission to the New Zealand Government," 2001) Shell stated: "Shell Petroleum Mining is of the view that business and investment confidence currently is and will continue to be adversely impacted by the current process of ratification followed by policy development." The Petroleum Exploration Group, of which Shell is a member, stated the following:

> The country is being asked to state a view on ratification of the Protocol in the absence of any detailed knowledge of the costs and benefits of doing so (or indeed of not doing so)—in other words, there has been no business case made for ratification, which given the potentially significant costs and wealth re-distribution effects of ratification (particularly in rural regions) seems extremely imprudent. ("Consultation Round One Submission to the New Zealand Government," 2001)

Together, these much less public actions and inactions by Shell suggest that although the company's responses to environmental concerns have had a material basis, they represent only small concessions.

---

[1]This major oil company is consistently referred to as BP, formerly known as British Petroleum.

Symmetrical Communication: In Whose Interest?

In each of the previous cases, as well as any others of symmetrical communication, further questions arise. In whose interests are concessions in policy made? By re-examining our examples it can be argued that the organizations that, from their dominant but challenged positions, make substantive changes to their practices, do so in order to maintain their existing hegemony. At one level, that hegemony is centered on practices within the organization. At another level, it is centered on the organization's relationships with organizations of other potential power blocs of society. In each case, the organizations are the subject of dissent from an active public sphere of civil society.

In the case of the WTO, the IMF, and the World Bank, the inclusion of NGOs and social movement representatives in policy discussions has not fundamentally changed their agenda of economic globalization. Inclusion of NGOs has been on a selective basis, with invitations issued to those groups that are acknowledged as "mainstream" and conservative. Mike Moore, former Director General of the WTO, stated that the WTO "should continue to respond to the legitimate expectations of civil society" (G7, 2001). His wording positions excluded groups as not legitimate, a limitation of symmetrical communication in practice specifically raised by Cheney and Christensen (2001).

The IMF believes that it can work with groups of civil society in an effort to educate citizens that structural adjustment works for the common good (O'Brien et al., 2000). The World Bank has continued to support private corporations in their investments, without, at the operational level, questioning the real value of those investments in developing countries. In effect, its macroeconomic prescriptions have not changed (Bello, 2000), and nor has the free market ideology that drives those prescriptions. By listening to the concerns of civil society and responding in a substantive manner to their demands for greater openness in decision making, the three MEIs could be said to communicating symmetrically. Does this make them "excellent" organizations? What they have attempted to do, in practice, is to make sufficient concession to deflect the more wide reaching opposition. As stated by O'Brien et al. (2000),

> In general, the goal of MEI interaction with GSMs [global social movements] is to neutralize their opposition so that the policy process can function smoothly. This goal is pursued in different forms and to different extents in the three institutions because of their distinct methods of operation and policy functions. (p. 217)

The case of Shell is amongst those that Levy (2001) used to demonstrate the business strategy of making concessions in order to maintain hegemony. Although Shell has committed large amounts of money to research and development of alternative energy sources, when weighed against its overall budget these amounts are small.

Although concessions have been made toward reducing carbon gas production, exploration for new sources of oil continues, along with a clear expectation that business will continue, for the most part, as usual. Had Shell not conceded the reality of the issue of climate change, opposition from the public sphere might have grown to such an extent that governments would have been forced into stringent regulations against them. As Levy said, "The companies seem to have concluded ... that open defiance of the climate-change consensus could jeopardize their long-run interests even more—causing them to lose political legitimacy and therefore the power to shape the eventual regulatory outcome" (p. 22).

In assessing whether an organization is exercising "excellent" public relations through a symmetrical approach to communication we also need to examine the extent of the concessions made to external stakeholders. Are they "just enough" to quiet public criticism, allowing essentially a business as usual strategy to remain in force? Are they allowing the continuing co-operation between business and government, preventing the introduction of unwelcome legislation—and at what price? It has long been considered that voluntary self-regulation by businesses, from an issues management perspective, is preferable to legislated regulation. Legislation alters the balance of power between the state and the economy. By sufficiently restoring legitimacy, organizations can prevent resisting groups from success in demands for more restrictive legislation. Levy (2001) cited a United Nations report that concludes that

> the most significant concern with some forms of voluntary initiatives and partnerships is that they may serve to weaken key drivers of corporate responsibility, namely governmental and inter-governmental regulation, the role of trade unions and collective bargaining, as well as more critical forms of NGO activism and civil society protest (p. 39).

J. E. Grunig acknowledged that "the symmetrical model actually serves the self-interest of the organization better than an asymmetrical model because 'organizations get more of what they want when they give up some of what they want'" (J. E. Grunig, 2001, p. 13; J. E. Grunig & White, 1992, p. 39). Symmetrical communication can be seen as an ongoing process rather than a one-off event. So, too, is hegemony, by definition. As stated earlier in this article, hegemony is maintained through a process of concessions to challenges at multiple points over time. However, Gramsci (1971) also pointed out that if hegemony is to be maintained, those concessions cannot fundamentally alter core power relationships:

> But there is ... no doubt that such sacrifices and such a compromise cannot touch the essential; for though hegemony is ethical-political, it must also be economic, must necessarily be based on the decisive function exercised by the leading groups in the decisive nucleus of economic activity. (p. 161)

Although it appears that whatever companies do they will be criticized for not doing enough, there are certainly positive aspects to the initiatives taken by Shell and by other similar companies such as BP. The changes in their behavior represent a welcome shift from total disregard of the impacts of their operations. However, is it honest for public relations practitioners, or theorists, to assert that such initiatives are taken in the spirit of open collaboration with all of their clients' stakeholders? What companies such as Shell are doing is negotiating through the making of compromises. As I have argued, these compromises, in the long term, favor the corporations much more than their critical stakeholders in civil society and can serve to dilute the negotiating power of those stakeholders. Negotiations of this nature are rarely, if ever, truly collaborative. Nor are they based on democratic principles of open debate regarding the public good, with special interests put aside. Can we legitimately call this "ethical" public relations?

ACKNOWLEDGMENT

I thank the Waikato Management School, University of Waikato, for funding the research component of this article.

REFERENCES

Barsamian, D. (1998, August 23). Challenging corporate power: An interview with Richard Grossman. *Zmagazine Online*. Retrieved September 7, 2000, from http://www.xmag.org/intgrossman.htm

Beder, S. (1997). *Global spin: The corporate assault on environmentalism*. Foxhole, England: Green.

Bello, W. (2000, September). Is the World Bank out of structural adjustment? *The Ecologist Report*, p. 11.

Bocock, R. (1986). *Hegemony*. New York: Tavistock.

Brown, L. (2000). *The rise and fall of the Global Climate Coalition* [Press release]. Worldwatch. Retrieved August 15, 2000, from http://www.worldwatch.org/chairman/issue/000725.html

Burchell, G. (1996). Liberal government and techniques of the self. In A. Barry, T. Osborne, & N. Rose (Eds.), *Foucault and political reason: Liberalism, neo-liberalism and rationalities of government* (pp. 19–36). London: UCL.

Castells, M. (2000). Information technology and global capitalism. In W. Hutton & A. Giddens (Eds.), *Global capitalism* (pp. 52–74). New York: New Press.

Chambers, W. B. (2001). International trade law and the Kyoto Protocol: Potential incompatibilities. In W. B. Chambers (Ed.), *Inter-linkages: The Kyoto Protocol and the international trade and investment regimes* (pp. 87–118). New York: United Nations University Press.

Cheney, G., & Christensen, L. (2001). Public relations as contested terrain: A critical response. In R. Heath (Ed.), *Handbook of public relations* (pp. 167–182). Thousand Oaks, CA: Sage.

Cohen, J., & Arato, A. (1992). *Civil society and political theory*. London: MIT Press.

Dahlgren, P. (1995). *Television and the public sphere*. London: Sage.

Eley, G. (1992). Nations, publics, and political cultures: Placing Habermas in the nineteenth century. In C. Calhoun (Ed.), *Habermas and the public sphere* (pp. 289–339). Cambridge, MA: MIT Press.

Elkington, J. (1999). Triple-bottom line reporting: Looking for balance. *Australian Accountant, 69*(2), 18–21.

Fairclough, N. (1989). *Language and power*. London: Longman.

Fairclough, N. (1992). *Discourse and social change*. Cambridge, England: Polity.

Fairclough, N. (1995). *Critical discourse analysis*. London: Longman.

G7. (2001). *G7 statement* [Joint statement]. Genoa summit. Retrieved September 5, 2001, from http://www.g8italia.it/_en/docs/JYTNI13F.htm

Gallhofer, S., Haslam, J., & Roper, J. (2001). Problematising finance in practice: A case study of struggles over takeovers legislation in New Zealand. *Advances in Accountability: Regulation, Research, Gender and Justice, 8*, 121–155.

Gandy, O. (1992). Public relations and public policy: The structuration of dominance in the information age. In E. Toth & R. Heath (Eds.), *Rhetorical and critical approaches to public relations* (pp. 131–164). Hillsdale, NJ: Lawrence Erlbaum Associates, Inc.

Giddens, A. (1998). *The third way: The renewal of social democracy*. Cambridge, England: Polity.

Giddens, A. (2000). *The third way and its critics*. Cambridge, England: Polity.

Gramsci, A. (1971). *Selections from the prison notebooks of Antonio Gramsci* (Q. Hoare & G. Nowell Smith, Trans.). New York: International.

Grossman, R. (1998). *Challenging corporate power* [Interview]. zmag. Retrieved September 7, 2000,from http://www.zmag.org/intgrossman.htm

Grunig, J. E. (1992). Communication, public relations, and effective organisations: An overview of the book. In J. E. Grunig (Ed.), *Excellence in public relations and communication management* (pp. 1–28). Hillsdale, NJ: Lawrence Erlbaum Associates, Inc.

Grunig, J. E. (2001). Two-way symmetrical public relations: Past, present, and future. In R. Heath (Ed.), *Handbook of public relations* (pp. 11–30). Thousand Oaks, CA: Sage.

Grunig, J. E., & Hunt, T. (1984). *Managing public relations*. New York: Holt, Rinehart & Winston.

Grunig, J. E., & White, J. (1992). The effect of worldviews on public relations theory and practice. In J. E. Grunig (Ed.), *Excellence in public relations and communication management* (pp. 31–64). Hillsdale, NJ: Lawrence Erlbaum Associates, Inc.

Habermas, J. (1974). *Theory and practice* (J. Viertel, Trans.). London: Heinemann.

Habermas, J. (1976). *Legitimation crisis* (T. McCarthy, Trans.). London: Heinemann.

Habermas, J. (1979). The public sphere (FRG, 1964). In A. Mattelart & S. Siegelaub (Eds.), *Communication & class struggle* (Vol. 1, pp. 198–201). New York: International General.

Habermas, J. (1987). *The theory of communicative action* (T. McCarthy, Trans., Vol. 2). Cambridge, England: Polity.

Habermas, J. (1991). *The structural transformation of the public sphere* (T. Burger, Trans.). Cambridge, MA: MIT Press.

Habermas, J. (1992). Further reflections on the public sphere. In C. Calhoun (Ed.), *Habermas and the public sphere* (pp. 421–461). Cambridge, MA: MIT Press.

Habermas, J. (1996). *Between facts and norms: Contributions to a discourse theory of law and democracy* (W. Rehg, Trans.). Cambridge, MA: MIT Press.

Hall, S. (1986). On postmodernism and articulation. *Journal of Communication Inquiry, 10*(2), 45–60.

Hall, S. (1988a). *The hard road to renewal. Thatcherism and the crisis of the left*. London: Verso.

Hall, S. (1988b). The toad in the garden: Thatcherism among the theorists. In C. Nelson & L. Grossberg (Eds.), *Marxism and the interpretation of culture* (pp. 35–57). London: MacMillian Education.

Heath, R. (1997). *Strategic issues management*. Thousand Oaks, CA: Sage.

Holub, R. (1992). *Antonio Gramsci: Beyond Marxism and postmodernism*. New York: Routledge.

Klein, N. (1999). *No logo*. New York: Picador.

Knight, P. (1998). *Profits and principles—Does there have to be a choice?* [Report]. London: Royal Dutch/Shell Group.

Kuttner, R. (2000). The role of governments in the global economy. In W. Hutton & A. Giddens (Eds.), *Global capitalism* (pp. 147–163). New York: New Press.

Leggett, J. (1999). *The carbon war: On the front lines of global warming at the end of the oil century.* London: Penguin.

Leitch, S., & Neilson, D. (2001). Bringing publics into public relations: New theoretical frameworks for practice. In R. Heath (Ed.), *Handbook of public relations* (pp. 127–138). Thousand Oaks, CA: Sage.

Levy, D. (1997). Environmental management as political sustainability. *Organization & Environment, 10,* 126–147.

Levy, D. (2001, January/February). Business and climate change. *Dollars and Sense,* pp. 21–23, 39.

Livesey, S. (2001). Eco-identity as discursive struggle: Royal Dutch/Shell, Brent Spar, and Nigeria. *Journal of Business Communication, 38*(1), 58–91.

Livesey, S., & Shearer, M. (2003, February 14–18). *Oil Industry Discourses on Climate Change: US and European Company Strategies.* Paper presented at the Western States Communication Association, Salt Lake City, Utah.

Maarek, P. (1995). *Political marketing and communication.* London: Libbey.

Mancini, P., & Swanson, D. (1996). Politics, media, and modern democracy: Introduction. In D. Swanson & P. Mancini (Eds.), *Politics, media, and modern democracy* (pp. 1–26). Westport, CT: Praeger.

Mayhew, L. (1997). *The new public: Professional communication and the means of social influence.* Cambridge, England: Cambridge University Press.

Motion, J., & Leitch, J. (1996). A discursive perspective from New Zealand: Another world view. *Public Relations Review, 22*(3), 297–309.

Motion, J., & Weaver, C. K. (2005/this issue). The discourse perspective for critical public relations research: Life Sciences Network and the battle for truth. *Journal of Public Relations Research, 17,* 49–67.

Murphy, P. (1991). The limits of symmetry: A game theory approach to symmetric and asymmetric public relations. In L. A. Grunig & J. E. Grunig (Eds.), *Public relations research annual* (Vol. 3, pp. 15–131). Hillsdale, NJ: Lawrence Erlbaum Association, Inc.

Newell, P. (2000). Environmental NGOs and globalization: The governance of TNCs. In R. Cohen & S. Rai (Eds.), *Global social movements* (pp. 117–133). London: Athlone.

Newman, B. (1994). *The marketing of the president: Political marketing as campaign strategy.* Thousand Oaks, CA: Sage.

O'Brien, R., Goetz, A. M., Scholte, J. A., & Williams, M. (2000). *Contesting global governance: Multilateral economic institutions and global social movements.* Cambridge, England: Cambridge University Press.

Roper, J. (2002). Government, corporate or social power? The Internet as a tool in the struggle for dominance in public policy. *Journal of Public Affairs, 2*(3), 113–124.

Roper, J., & Collins, E. (2003, February 14–18). *Business, climate change policy and sustainability.* Paper presented at the Western States Communication Association, Salt Lake City, Utah.

Shell Oil Co. (2001, December 18). *Consultation round one submission to the New Zealand government.* Unpublished submission to the New Zealand Government.

Yearley, S., & Forrester, J. (2000). Shell, a sure target for global environmental campaigning? In R. Cohen & S. Rai (Eds.), *Global social movements* (pp. 134–145). London: Athlone.